Canadian Living
Make It Ahead!

EXCLUSIVE DISTRIBUTOR FOR CANADA & USA
Simon & Schuster Canada
166 King Street East, Suite 300
Toronto ON M5A 1J3
Tel: 647-427-8882
Toll Free: 800-387-0446
Fax: 647-430-9446

simonandschuster.ca   canadianliving.com/books

Cataloguing data available from
Bibliothèque et Archives nationales du Québec.

Art director and project manager: Colin Elliott
Project editor: Martin Zibauer
Copy editor: Ruth Hanley
Indexer: Beth Zablowski

07-16

Legal deposit: 2016
Bibliothèque et Archives nationales du Québec
Library and Archives Canada

ISBN 978-1-988002-27-9

Printed in Canada

Government of Quebec – Tax credit for book publishing –
Administered by SODEC.
sodec.gouv.qc.ca

This publisher gratefully acknowledges the support of the
Société de développement des enterprises culturelles du Québec.

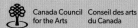

Canada Council   Conseil des arts
for the Arts   du Canada

We gratefully acknowledge the support of the
Canada Council for the Arts for its publishing program.

We acknowledge the financial support of our publishing activities
by the Government of Canada through the Canada Book Fund.

Canadian Living
Make It Ahead!

BY THE CANADIAN LIVING TEST KITCHEN

JUNIPER
PUBLISHING
A Quebecor Media Corporation

WELCOME TO THE
Canadian Living Test Kitchen

You love to cook, and we want you to feel great about every meal that comes out of your kitchen — so creating delicious, trustworthy recipes is the top priority for us in the Canadian Living Test Kitchen. We are chefs, recipe developers and food writers, all from different backgrounds but equally dedicated to the art and science of creating delicious recipes you can make right at home.

What Does Tested Till Perfect Mean?

Every year, the food specialists in the Canadian Living Test Kitchen work together to produce approximately 500 Tested-Till-Perfect recipes. So what does Tested Till Perfect mean? It means we follow a rigorous process to ensure you'll get the same results in your kitchen as we do in ours.

Here's What We Do:

- In the Test Kitchen, we use the same everyday ingredients and equipment that you use in your own kitchen.
- We start by researching ideas and brainstorming as a team.
- We write up the recipe and go straight into the kitchen to try it out.
- We taste, evaluate and tweak the recipe until we really love it.
- Each recipe then gets handed off to different food editors for another test and another tasting session.
- We meticulously test and retest each recipe as many times as it takes to make sure it turns out as perfectly in your kitchen as it does in ours.
- We carefully weigh and measure all ingredients, record the data and send the recipe out for nutritional analysis.
- The recipe is then edited and rechecked to ensure all the information is correct and it's ready for you to cook.

Our Tested-Till-Perfect guarantee means we've tested every recipe, using the same grocery store ingredients and household appliances as you do, until we're sure you'll get perfect results at home.

Contents

◄ Chocolate Caramel
Cupcake Parfaits
page 151

Mini Smoked Salmon Dill Quiches

HANDS-ON TIME	•	TOTAL TIME	•	MAKES
30 MINUTES		2 HOURS		24 PIECES

What you need

How to make it

SOUR CREAM PASTRY
2½ cups	all-purpose flour
½ tsp	salt
½ cup	each cold butter and cold lard, cubed
¼ cup	ice water
3 tbsp	sour cream

FILLING
170 g	smoked salmon, chopped
half	pkg (250 g pkg) cream cheese, diced
4	eggs
1	cup milk
2½ tbsp	chopped fresh dill
2	green onions, minced
¼ tsp	each salt and pepper

SOUR CREAM PASTRY: In large bowl, whisk flour with salt. Using pastry blender or 2 knives, cut in butter and lard until mixture resembles fine crumbs with a few larger pieces. Whisk ice water with sour cream; drizzle over flour mixture, stirring briskly with fork until ragged dough forms. Divide in half; shape into discs. Wrap each in plastic wrap; refrigerate until chilled, about 30 minutes. (Make-ahead: Refrigerate for up to 3 days.)

On floured work surface, roll out pastry to generous ⅛-inch (3 mm) thickness. Using 4-inch (10 cm) round pastry cutter, cut out 24 rounds, rerolling scraps as necessary. Arrange 1 round in each of 24 wells of muffin pans, leaving overhang. Prick all over with fork. Place on rimmed baking sheets; refrigerate for 30 minutes. Line shells with foil; fill with pie weights or dried beans. Bake on bottom rack in 400°F (200°C) oven until rims are light golden, about 10 minutes. Remove weights and foil; let cool in pans on racks.

FILLING: Sprinkle salmon and cream cheese into shells. Whisk together eggs, milk, dill, green onions, salt and pepper; pour into shells.

Bake in 375°F (190°C) oven until knife inserted into several quiches comes out clean, about 20 minutes. Let cool in pans on racks for 5 minutes. (Make-ahead: Let cool. Layer between waxed paper in airtight container; refrigerate for up to 24 hours or freeze for up to 2 weeks. Thaw if frozen; reheat in 350°F/180°C oven for 10 minutes.)

NUTRITIONAL INFORMATION, PER PIECE: about 151 cal, 4 g pro, 11 g total fat (5 g sat. fat), 9 g carb (trace dietary fibre), 52 mg chol, 177 mg sodium, 63 mg potassium. % RDI: 2% calcium, 6% iron, 7% vit A, 13% folate.

Lemon Herb Chicken Pops

HANDS-ON TIME	TOTAL TIME	MAKES
30 MINUTES	1½ HOURS	ABOUT 30 PIECES

What you need

⅓ cup	olive oil
1 tbsp	grated lemon zest
¼ cup	lemon juice
2	cloves garlic, minced
2 tsp	each dried basil and dried rosemary
1 tsp	each salt and dried thyme
½ tsp	pepper
4	boneless skinless chicken breasts, cut in 1½-inch (4 cm) cubes

How to make it

In large bowl, whisk together oil, lemon zest, lemon juice, garlic, basil, rosemary, salt, thyme and pepper. Add chicken; toss to coat. Cover and refrigerate for 1 hour. *(Make-ahead: Refrigerate for up to 4 hours.)*

Thread 1 piece of chicken onto each of 30 metal or soaked wooden cocktail skewers. *(Make-ahead: Freeze on waxed paper–lined baking sheet until firm, about 2 hours. Transfer to airtight container; freeze for up to 2 weeks. Cook from frozen, adding 4 minutes to cook time.)* In grill pan or skillet and working in batches, cook chicken skewers over medium heat, turning once, until chicken is golden and no longer pink inside, about 6 minutes.

TIP FROM THE TEST KITCHEN
Look for cocktail skewers at kitchen supply stores.

NUTRITIONAL INFORMATION, PER PIECE: about 20 cal, 2 g pro, 1 g total fat (trace sat. fat), trace carb (0 g dietary fibre), 4 mg chol, 45 mg sodium. % RDI: 1% iron, 2% vit C.

Savoury Cheddar Cheesecake Spread

p.158

HANDS-ON TIME	•	TOTAL TIME	•	MAKES
20 MINUTES		4½ HOURS		ABOUT 2 CUPS

What you need

1	pkg (250 g) cream cheese, softened
1	egg
½ cup	shredded old Cheddar cheese
1	shallot, grated
¼ tsp	each cayenne pepper and smoked paprika
½ cup	chopped toasted pecans
½ cup	peach chutney

How to make it

In bowl, beat cream cheese until smooth. On low speed, beat in egg, beating well and scraping down side of bowl often. Beat in Cheddar, shallot, cayenne pepper and smoked paprika.

In bowl, stir pecans with chutney; stir half of pecan mixture into the cream cheese mixture. Scrape into parchment paper–lined 5-inch (600 mL) springform pan. Spread remaining pecan mixture on top. Centre pan on large square of foil; press foil up against side of pan.

Set springform pan in larger pan; pour enough hot water into larger pan to come 1 inch (2.5 cm) up sides. Bake in 300°F (150°C) oven until no longer shiny and edge is set yet centre still jiggles slightly, about 1¼ hours. Turn off oven. Immediately run knife around edge of cheesecake. Let cool in oven for 1 hour.

Remove springform pan from water and transfer to rack; remove foil and let cool completely. Refrigerate until chilled and set, about 2 hours. *(Make-ahead: Cover and refrigerate for up to 4 days.)*

TIP FROM THE TEST KITCHEN

Be sure to bake the cheesecake spread in a water bath; this ensures even and slow cooking. Wrapping the springform pan in foil prevents any water from seeping into the pan.

NUTRITIONAL INFORMATION, PER 1 TBSP: about 57 cal, 1 g pro, 5 g total fat (2 g sat. fat), 3 g carb (trace dietary fibre, 3 g sugar), 16 mg chol, 90 mg sodium, 26 mg potassium. % RDI: 2% calcium, 1% iron, 4% vit A, 1% folate.

Mini Potato and Zucchini Latkes

HANDS-ON TIME	TOTAL TIME	MAKES
50 MINUTES	1¼ HOURS	ABOUT 40 PIECES

What you need

250 g	zucchini (about 2 small)
½ tsp	salt
450 g	yellow-fleshed potatoes (about 3), peeled
half	onion, grated
1	egg, lightly beaten
3 tbsp	all-purpose flour
	vegetable oil for frying

How to make it

Using grater or food processor with shredder blade, coarsely grate zucchini. Transfer to colander; sprinkle with half of the salt. Let stand for 30 minutes. Using tea towel or potato ricer, squeeze out and discard liquid. Transfer zucchini to large bowl.

Meanwhile, using grater or food processor with shredder blade, coarsely grate potatoes. Using tea towel or potato ricer, squeeze out and discard liquid. Add potatoes to bowl with zucchini. Using fork, mix in onion, egg, flour and remaining salt.

In large skillet, add enough oil to cover bottom of pan; heat over medium-high heat. Working in batches, drop zucchini mixture by rounded 1 tbsp into skillet, flattening slightly and leaving at least 1 inch (2.5 cm) between each. Cook, turning halfway through and adding more oil as needed, until golden and edges are crisp, about 5 minutes. Transfer to paper towel–lined racks to drain. *(Make-ahead: Remove paper towels; let stand on racks for up to 4 hours, or cover and refrigerate on racks for up to 24 hours. Reheat on racks on baking sheets in 425°F/220°C oven for 6 to 8 minutes.)*

Chunky Applesauce

In saucepan, combine 4 apples, peeled, cored and chopped; ½ cup apple cider or water; and ¼ cup granulated sugar. Bring to boil over medium heat. Reduce heat to simmer; cover and cook, stirring, until apples are tender, about 25 minutes. Using potato masher, mash until chunky. Stir in 1 tbsp lemon juice. Let cool to room temperature. *(Make-ahead: Refrigerate in airtight container for up to 3 days.)* Serve with latkes.

MAKES ABOUT 2 CUPS

NUTRITIONAL INFORMATION, PER PIECE: about 36 cal, trace pro, 2 g total fat (trace sat. fat), 4 g carb (trace dietary fibre), 0 mg chol, 16 mg sodium, 60 mg potassium. % RDI: 1% iron, 1% vit A, 2% vit C, 2% folate.

Fried Tofu
With Spicy Sesame Dipping Sauce

HANDS-ON TIME	•	TOTAL TIME	•	MAKES
35 MINUTES		1 HOUR		ABOUT 30 PIECES

What you need

FRIED TOFU
1	pkg (454 g) firm tofu
¼ cup	vegetable oil

SPICY SESAME DIPPING SAUCE
¼ cup	sodium-reduced soy sauce
2 tbsp	minced green onion
2 tbsp	rice vinegar
2	cloves garlic, minced
2 tsp	sesame seeds, toasted
2 tsp	sesame oil
1 tsp	hot pepper flakes
½ tsp	granulated sugar

How to make it

FRIED TOFU: Cut tofu into 1-inch (2.5 cm) cubes. Let stand on plate for 30 minutes; discard liquid. In skillet, heat oil over medium-high heat; working in batches, cook tofu, turning often, until golden brown, 5 to 7 minutes. Transfer to paper towel–lined plate to drain. *(Make-ahead: Cover and refrigerate for up to 24 hours. Bring to room temperature before serving.)*

SPICY SESAME DIPPING SAUCE: In bowl, mix together soy sauce, green onion, vinegar, garlic, sesame seeds, sesame oil, hot pepper flakes and sugar. Serve with tofu.

NUTRITIONAL INFORMATION, PER PIECE: about 25 cal, 2 g pro, 2 g total fat (trace sat. fat), 1 g carb (trace dietary fibre), 0 mg chol, 140 mg sodium. % RDI: 3% calcium, 2% iron, 2% vit A, 3% vit C, 3% folate.

Cheeseburger Spring Rolls

HANDS-ON TIME	•	TOTAL TIME	•	MAKES
40 MINUTES		1 HOUR		32 PIECES

What you need

1 tsp	olive oil
1 cup	diced red onion
2	cloves garlic, minced
225 g	lean ground beef
1 cup	cubed processed cheese product (such as Velveeta)
1 cup	fresh bread crumbs
¼ cup	diced dill pickle, patted dry
2	green onions, chopped
1 tbsp	yellow mustard
1 tsp	Worcestershire sauce
½ tsp	pepper
64	spring roll wrappers
1	egg

How to make it

In skillet, heat oil over medium heat; cook red onion and garlic, stirring occasionally, until softened, about 5 minutes.

Add beef; cook, breaking up with spoon, until browned, about 4 minutes. Drain well; return to pan. Stir in cheese; cook over medium heat until cheese is melted, about 2 minutes. Scrape into bowl.

Stir bread crumbs, pickle, green onions, mustard, Worcestershire sauce and pepper into beef mixture; let cool for about 15 minutes.

Layer 2 spring roll wrappers on work surface with point facing up; place 1 tbsp beef mixture on bottom third of wrapper. Fold bottom corner of wrapper over filling. Fold in sides and roll up until 2-inch (5 cm) triangle of wrapper remains at top. Mix egg with 2 tsp water; lightly brush over triangle and loosely roll up to seal. Repeat with remaining beef mixture, wrappers and egg mixture.

Place rolls, seam side down, on parchment paper–lined baking sheet. *(Make-ahead: Cover and refrigerate for up to 12 hours; bake as directed. Or freeze on baking sheet for 1 hour; transfer to airtight container and freeze for up to 2 weeks. Bake in 350°F/180°C oven for 30 minutes.)* Bake in 375°F (190°C) oven, turning once, until light golden, about 25 minutes.

TIP FROM THE TEST KITCHEN
Doubling up the spring roll wrappers provides extra crunch and helps prevent the filling from bursting out.

NUTRITIONAL INFORMATION, PER PIECE: about 124 cal, 5 g pro, 3 g total fat (2 g sat. fat), 18 g carb (trace dietary fibre, 1 g sugar), 12 mg chol, 218 mg sodium, 36 mg potassium. % RDI: 2% calcium, 1% iron, 1% vit A, 1% folate.

Lemon Pepper Salmon Cakes With Herbed Garlic Mayo

HANDS-ON TIME	•	TOTAL TIME	•	MAKES
1 HOUR		1 HOUR		ABOUT 30 PIECES

What you need

How to make it

SALMON CAKES

450 g	yellow-fleshed potatoes (about 2 large), peeled and halved
¼ cup	dried bread crumbs
2	green onions, chopped
¼ cup	chopped fresh parsley
½ tsp	grated lemon zest
2 tbsp	lemon juice
2	cloves garlic, minced
½ tsp	each salt and pepper
1	egg, lightly beaten
2	cans (each 213 g) red sockeye salmon, drained and flaked
2 tbsp	vegetable oil

HERBED GARLIC MAYO

½ cup	light mayonnaise
1 tbsp	chopped fresh parsley
1	clove garlic, minced
½ tsp	grated lemon zest

SALMON CAKES: In saucepan of boiling salted water, cook potatoes, covered, until tender, about 15 minutes. Drain and return to pan; using potato masher, mash until smooth.

In large bowl, stir together potatoes, bread crumbs, green onions, parsley, lemon zest, lemon juice, garlic, salt and pepper; stir in egg. Fold in salmon. Let cool for 5 minutes. Shape by rounded 1 tbsp into ¼-inch (5 mm) thick patties. *(Make-ahead: Arrange in single layer on waxed paper–lined baking sheet; cover and refrigerate for up to 24 hours.)*

In large nonstick skillet, heat oil over medium heat; working in batches, cook patties, turning once, until golden, about 8 minutes. *(Make-ahead: Cover and refrigerate on foil-lined baking sheet for up to 24 hours. Reheat in 375°F/190°C oven for about 6 minutes.)*

HERBED GARLIC MAYO: Meanwhile, in bowl, stir together mayonnaise, parsley, garlic and lemon zest. *(Make-ahead: Cover and refrigerate for up to 2 days.)* Serve with salmon cakes.

TIP FROM THE TEST KITCHEN
You can use canned tuna, shrimp or crab, or 1¾ cups flaked cooked fish instead of canned salmon.

NUTRITIONAL INFORMATION, PER PIECE: about 50 cal, 3 g pro, 3 g total fat (trace sat. fat), 3 g carb (trace dietary fibre), 10 mg chol, 142 mg sodium. % RDI: 3% calcium, 2% iron, 1% vit A, 3% vit C, 2% folate.

SERVING SUGGESTION

Serve this **Chive and Garlic Cheese Spread** with crisp crackers, warm biscuits and vegetable crudités.

Chive and Garlic Cheese Spread

HANDS-ON TIME		TOTAL TIME		MAKES
15 MINUTES	•	2¼ HOURS	•	ABOUT 2 CUPS

What you need

2 cups	shredded Havarti cheese
1	pkg (250 g) cream cheese, softened
2 tbsp	whipping cream (35%)
1	small clove garlic, chopped
½ tsp	dry mustard
¼ tsp	pepper
3 tbsp	chopped fresh chives
4 tsp	chopped fresh parsley

How to make it

In food processor, purée together Havarti, cream cheese, cream, garlic, mustard and pepper until smooth; stir in chives and parsley.

Line small, deep bowl with plastic wrap; scrape in Havarti mixture, pressing firmly and smoothing top. Cover and refrigerate until firm, about 2 hours. *(Make-ahead: Refrigerate in airtight container for up to 5 days.)*

Unwrap cheese ball and invert onto serving plate.

TIP FROM THE TEST KITCHEN

You'll need a bowl that holds at least 2 cups to fit the cheese mixture. If you're not sure of your bowl's capacity, measure 2 cups of water and pour it in to check.

NUTRITIONAL INFORMATION, PER 1 TBSP: about 60 cal, 2 g pro, 6 g total fat (3 g sat. fat), trace carb (0 g dietary fibre, trace sugar), 18 mg chol, 79 mg sodium, 14 mg potassium. % RDI: 5% calcium, 1% iron, 5% vit A.

Bite-Size Shrimp Frittatas

HANDS-ON TIME	•	TOTAL TIME	•	MAKES
15 MINUTES		30 MINUTES		16 PIECES

What you need

8	eggs
½ cup	sliced green onions
2 tbsp	grated Parmesan cheese
1 tbsp	all-purpose flour
1 tsp	baking powder
pinch	each salt and pepper
1 cup	cooked deveined peeled salad shrimp, patted dry

How to make it

In bowl, whisk together eggs, green onions, Parmesan, flour, baking powder, salt and pepper. Spoon scant 2 tbsp of the mixture into each of 16 greased wells of nonstick muffin pans. Spoon 1 tbsp of the shrimp into centre of each well.

Bake in 350°F (180°C) oven until tip of knife inserted into several frittatas comes out clean, about 15 minutes. Let cool in pans for 1 minute; transfer to racks and let cool completely. (*Make-ahead: Refrigerate in airtight container for up to 24 hours. Reheat on baking sheet in 350°F/180°C oven for 10 minutes.*)

TIP FROM THE TEST KITCHEN
Salad shrimp are tiny—there are 100 to 150 in 450 g. Any extra-small canned or frozen shrimp will work in these frittatas. You can also use larger shrimp; just chop them coarsely for this recipe.

NUTRITIONAL INFORMATION, PER PIECE: about 51 cal, 5 g pro, 3 g total fat (1 g sat. fat), 1 g carb (trace dietary fibre), 109 mg chol, 80 mg sodium, 56 mg potassium. % RDI: 3% calcium, 4% iron, 4% vit A, 2% vit C, 7% folate.

Lamb Sausage Rolls

HANDS-ON TIME	•	TOTAL TIME	•	MAKES
35 MINUTES		1¼ HOURS		60 PIECES

What you need

2	eggs
¼ cup	fresh bread crumbs, toasted
¼ cup	minced onion
1	clove garlic, minced
2 tbsp	chopped fresh parsley
2 tsp	crushed fennel seeds
1 tsp	grated orange zest
½ tsp	each salt and ground coriander
¼ tsp	pepper
450 g	ground lamb
2	sheets (450 g pkg) frozen butter puff pastry, thawed
2 tbsp	Dijon mustard
1	egg yolk

How to make it

In large bowl, mix together eggs, bread crumbs, onion, garlic, parsley, fennel seeds, orange zest, salt, coriander and pepper; stir in lamb. Set aside.

On lightly floured work surface, roll out 1 sheet of the pastry into 10-inch (25 cm) square; slice into 3 equal strips. Brush 1 tsp of the mustard over each strip. Spoon one-sixth of the lamb mixture along centre of each strip. Fold pastry lengthwise over filling; press edges to seal. Repeat with remaining pastry, mustard and lamb mixture.

Arrange, seam side down, on parchment paper–lined baking sheets. Cover and refrigerate until firm, about 25 minutes. Cut each roll crosswise into 10 pieces; arrange 1 inch (2.5 cm) apart on baking sheets. *(Make-ahead: Layer between waxed paper in airtight container; freeze for up to 2 weeks. Bake from frozen, adding 5 minutes to bake time.)*

Whisk egg yolk with 1 tbsp water; brush over rolls. Bake in 400°F (200°C) oven until puffed and golden, about 15 minutes.

TIP FROM THE TEST KITCHEN

For best results, thaw frozen puff pastry in the refrigerator overnight. If you prefer, you can substitute lean ground beef for the lamb.

NUTRITIONAL INFORMATION, PER PIECE: about 66 cal, 2 g pro, 5 g total fat (3 g sat. fat), 3 g carb (trace dietary fibre), 23 mg chol, 63 mg sodium. % RDI: 1% calcium, 3% iron, 3% vit A, 5% folate.

Crab and Three-Cheese Fondue

HANDS-ON TIME	•	TOTAL TIME	•	MAKES
25 MINUTES		30 MINUTES		ABOUT 3½ CUPS

What you need

280 g	Brie or Camembert cheese
1	pkg (250 g) cream cheese
2	pkg (each 212 g) pasteurized crabmeat
1 tbsp	butter
6	green onions, thinly sliced
1	clove garlic, minced
½ cup	whipping cream (35%)
¼ cup	dry white wine
1 tbsp	Dijon mustard
½ tsp	hot pepper sauce
½ cup	grated Parmesan cheese

How to make it

Cut off rind from Brie; chop Brie and cream cheese into small cubes. Cover and set aside until room temperature, about 20 minutes.

Meanwhile, pick through crabmeat to remove any shells or cartilage; drain, pressing to remove as much liquid as possible. Set aside.

In large skillet, melt butter over medium heat; cook green onions and garlic, stirring often, until softened, about 5 minutes.

Stir in Brie, cream cheese, cream, wine, mustard and hot pepper sauce; cook, mashing with back of spoon and stirring constantly, just until melted.

Remove from heat; stir in crabmeat and Parmesan. *(Make-ahead: Let cool. Cover and refrigerate for up to 24 hours. Reheat over medium-low.)* Scrape into fondue pot. Keep warm on low or medium-low setting.

TIP FROM THE TEST KITCHEN

Whether your fondue pot is electric or uses a fondue burner, adjust the heat to low or medium-low to prevent the mixture from sticking to the bottom. You can also use a small slow cooker on low to keep the fondue warm.

NUTRITIONAL INFORMATION, PER 1 TBSP: about 47 cal, 3 g pro, 4 g total fat (2 g sat. fat), trace carb (0 g dietary fibre), 16 mg chol, 107 mg sodium. % RDI: 2% calcium, 2% iron, 4% vit A, 2% folate.

SERVING SUGGESTION

For fun, casual entertaining, serve this **Crab and Three-Cheese Fondue** with crackers, flatbread or toasted slices of French bread alongside **Artichoke and Green Olive Dip** (recipe, page 22) and **Marinated Bocconcini** (recipe, page 25). All three recipes can be made a day or two before the party, so you can relax.

Artichoke and Green Olive Dip

p.21

| **HANDS-ON TIME**
15 MINUTES | • | **TOTAL TIME**
1¼ HOURS | • | **MAKES ABOUT**
2½ CUPS |

What you need

2	cans (each 400 mL) artichoke hearts, drained and rinsed
⅓ cup	pitted brine-cured green olives
⅓ cup	extra-virgin olive oil
2 tbsp	chopped fresh parsley
1 tbsp	lemon juice
1	clove garlic, minced
¼ tsp	pepper
pinch	hot pepper flakes (optional)

How to make it

In food processor, purée together artichokes, olives, oil, all but 1 tsp of the parsley, the lemon juice, garlic, pepper and hot pepper flakes (if using). Scrape into serving bowl; cover and refrigerate for 1 hour. *(Make-ahead: Refrigerate for up to 3 days.)* Sprinkle with remaining parsley.

Pita Chips

Using scissors, split four 8-inch (20 cm) pita pockets horizontally to make 8 rounds; cut each round into 8 triangles. In large bowl, toss together pita triangles, 2 tbsp vegetable oil and ¼ tsp salt. Spread on 2 rimmed baking sheets; bake in top and bottom thirds of 350°F (180°C) oven until crisp and golden, about 8 minutes. *(Make-ahead: Let cool; store in airtight container for up to 2 days.)*

MAKES 24 CHIPS

TIP FROM THE TEST KITCHEN
Serve this dip with pita chips, crudité, crackers, toasted baguette or flatbread.

NUTRITIONAL INFORMATION, PER 1 TBSP: about 24 cal, trace pro, 2 g total fat (trace sat. fat), 2 g carb (1 g dietary fibre), 0 mg chol, 30 mg sodium. % RDI: 1% calcium, 1% iron, 3% vit C, 3% folate.

Warm Mixed Olives and Chorizo

HANDS-ON TIME	•	TOTAL TIME	•	MAKES
15 MINUTES		25 MINUTES		ABOUT 4 CUPS

What you need

2 tbsp	olive oil
125 g	smoked chorizo or other smoked sausage, thinly sliced
1 cup	unpitted brined black olives (such as Kalamata)
1 cup	unpitted oil-cured black olives
1 cup	unpitted large green olives
2	cloves garlic, thinly sliced
1 tsp	hot pepper flakes
half	small navel orange, thinly sliced
1 tbsp	thinly sliced fresh sage leaves

How to make it

In large skillet, heat oil over medium heat; cook chorizo, stirring, for 1 minute.

Add brined black olives, oil-cured black olives, green olives, garlic and hot pepper flakes; cook, stirring occasionally, until heated through and fragrant, about 3 minutes.

Stir in orange and sage; cook until orange begins to break down, about 2 minutes. Remove from heat; cover and let stand for 10 minutes. Serve warm. *(Make-ahead: Cover and refrigerate for up to 3 days; reheat before serving.)*

TIP FROM THE TEST KITCHEN

You can use any kind of unpitted green and black olives in this Mediterranean-inspired warm appetizer. (Unpitted olives have better flavour and texture than pitted olives.) Serve with cocktail picks.

NUTRITIONAL INFORMATION, PER 2 TBSP: about 61 cal, 1 g pro, 6 g total fat (1 g sat. fat), 2 g carb (1 g dietary fibre), 3 mg chol, 393 mg sodium, 27 mg potassium. % RDI: 1% calcium, 1% iron, 1% vit A, 3% vit C.

Mustard-Spiced Nuts

HANDS-ON TIME	•	TOTAL TIME	•	MAKES
10 MINUTES		30 MINUTES		ABOUT 4 CUPS

What you need

1 cup	natural (skin-on) almonds
1 cup	raw cashews
1 cup	shelled pistachios
1 cup	walnut halves
1 tbsp	olive oil
1 tbsp	Dijon mustard
2 tbsp	packed brown sugar
1 tbsp	dry mustard
1½ tsp	ground coriander
1 tsp	salt
½ tsp	cayenne pepper
¼ tsp	pepper

How to make it

In bowl, stir together almonds, cashews, pistachios, walnuts, oil and Dijon mustard. In separate bowl, mix together brown sugar, dry mustard, coriander, salt, cayenne pepper and pepper; toss with nut mixture to coat.

Spread on parchment paper–lined baking sheet; bake in 350°F (180°C) oven, stirring once, until fragrant and lightly toasted, about 20 minutes. *(Make-ahead: Store in airtight container for up to 1 week.)*

TIP FROM THE TEST KITCHEN
Switch up the nuts according to your taste—just keep the total amount at 4 cups.

NUTRITIONAL INFORMATION, PER 2 TBSP: about 101 cal, 3 g pro, 8 g total fat (1 g sat. fat), 5 g carb (1 g dietary fibre), 0 mg chol, 79 mg sodium, 120 mg potassium. % RDI: 2% calcium, 6% iron, 4% folate.

Marinated Bocconcini

p.21

HANDS-ON TIME		TOTAL TIME		MAKES ABOUT
15 MINUTES	•	12¼ HOURS	•	4 CUPS

What you need

¾ cup	extra-virgin olive oil
1 tbsp	white wine vinegar
1	clove garlic, minced
½ tsp	Italian herb seasoning
¼ tsp	each salt and hot pepper flakes
4 cups	bocconcini cheese balls, each 1-inch (2.5 cm), drained (about 675 g)

How to make it

In bowl, whisk together oil, vinegar, garlic, Italian seasoning, salt and hot pepper flakes.

Fill two 2-cup (500 ml) jars with bocconcini; pour oil mixture over top. Seal and shake to coat.

Refrigerate for 12 hours. *(Make-ahead: Refrigerate for up to 5 days.)* Bring to room temperature; drain before serving.

TIP FROM THE TEST KITCHEN

Bocconcini comes in a few different sizes; 1-inch (2.5 cm) balls are ideal for this recipe. If you can only find larger bocconcini, cut them into quarters. Don't worry if the oil solidifies in the fridge; it will liquefy as it comes to room temperature.

NUTRITIONAL INFORMATION, PER PIECE: about 40 cal, 3 g pro, 3 g total fat (2 g sat. fat), trace carb (0 g dietary fibre), 10 mg chol, 53 mg sodium. % RDI: 7% calcium, 2% vit A.

Chilled Pea and Mint Soup

HANDS-ON TIME
20 MINUTES

•

TOTAL TIME
2½ HOURS

•

MAKES
8 TO 10 SERVINGS

What you need

2 tbsp	butter
2	leeks (white and light green parts only), thinly sliced
5 cups	frozen peas
1	pkg (900 mL) sodium-reduced chicken broth or vegetable broth
½ tsp	salt
¼ tsp	pepper
¼ cup	packed fresh mint leaves
½ cup	crème fraîche
3 tbsp	finely chopped fresh chives

How to make it

In Dutch oven or large heavy-bottomed saucepan, melt butter over medium heat; cook leeks, stirring occasionally, until softened, about 5 minutes.

Stir in peas, broth, salt, pepper and 2 cups water; bring to boil. Reduce heat to simmer; cook until peas are soft, about 10 minutes. Stir in mint.

In blender, working in batches, purée soup until smooth. Refrigerate until chilled, about 2 hours. *(Make-ahead: Refrigerate in airtight container for up to 24 hours.)*

Ladle into serving bowls; spoon crème fraîche onto soup. Sprinkle with chives.

TIP FROM THE TEST KITCHEN
As a leek grows, dirt and sand can get trapped between its layers. After trimming the dark green tops (save them to flavour homemade stock) and the root end, cut the leek lengthwise. Rinse it under running water, fanning the layers to get out any dirt.

NUTRITIONAL INFORMATION, PER EACH OF 10 SERVINGS:
about 134 cal, 5 g pro, 7 g total fat (5 g sat. fat), 12 g carb (3 g dietary fibre, 4 g sugar), 26 mg chol, 411 mg sodium, 111 mg potassium. % RDI: 3% calcium, 11% iron, 27% vit A, 15% vit C, 22% folate.

Broccoli Soup
With Cheddar Croutons

HANDS-ON TIME	•	TOTAL TIME	•	MAKES
35 MINUTES		40 MINUTES		6 TO 8 SERVINGS

What you need

How to make it

BROCCOLI SOUP

1	large head broccoli
1 tbsp	butter
3	leeks (white and light green parts only), sliced
450 g	yellow-fleshed potatoes (about 3), peeled and cut in ½-inch (1 cm) cubes
4	cloves garlic, sliced
1 tsp	dry mustard
¾ tsp	dried savory
1	pkg (900 mL) sodium-reduced vegetable broth
1 cup	shredded extra-old white Cheddar cheese
¼ cup	chopped fresh parsley
½ cup	sour cream
½ tsp	each salt and pepper

CHEDDAR CROUTONS

3 cups	cubed (½ inch/1 cm) baguette (about one-third baguette)
2 tsp	olive oil
½ cup	shredded extra-old white Cheddar cheese

BROCCOLI SOUP: Cut stem from broccoli head; cut head into florets to yield 5 cups. Trim bottom end from stem; peel outer layer of stem. Slice to yield ¾ cup. Set aside.

In Dutch oven or large heavy-bottomed saucepan, melt butter over medium heat; cook leeks, potatoes and broccoli stem, stirring occasionally, until leeks are softened, about 12 minutes. Add garlic, mustard and savory; cook, stirring, until fragrant, about 1 minute.

Stir in broth and 2 cups water; bring to boil. Reduce heat to simmer; cook for 5 minutes. Stir in broccoli florets; simmer until broccoli stems and potatoes are tender, about 8 minutes. Stir in Cheddar until melted; stir in parsley.

In blender, working in batches, purée soup until smooth. Pour into clean Dutch oven or large saucepan; heat over medium-low heat. Whisk in sour cream, salt and pepper; cook until heated through. *(Make-ahead: Refrigerate in airtight container for up to 2 days or freeze for up to 2 weeks.)*

CHEDDAR CROUTONS: While soup is simmering, in bowl, toss bread cubes with oil to coat. Arrange in single layer on parchment paper–lined rimmed baking sheet; sprinkle with Cheddar. Bake in 400°F (200°C) oven, turning once, until baguette is golden and Cheddar is melted, about 10 minutes. Break apart croutons; serve over soup.

TIP FROM THE TEST KITCHEN
When blending a hot soup, it's safest to work in small batches. Remove the vent from your blender lid to relieve any pressure caused by steam; cover the hole with a folded tea towel.

NUTRITIONAL INFORMATION, PER EACH OF 8 SERVINGS:
about 279 cal, 11 g pro, 13 g total fat (7 g sat. fat), 32 g carb (4 g dietary fibre, 5 g sugar), 31 mg chol, 31 mg sodium, 550 mg potassium. % RDI: 24% calcium, 21% iron, 36% vit A, 72% vit C, 43% folate.

Asparagus Soup With Thick Cream

HANDS-ON TIME	•	TOTAL TIME	•	MAKES
20 MINUTES		20 MINUTES		8 SERVINGS

What you need	How to make it

What you need

2 tsp	olive oil
4	cloves garlic, chopped
2	bunches (each about 450 g) asparagus, trimmed and cut in 1-inch (2.5 cm) lengths
2 cups	shelled fresh green peas
1	pkg (900 mL) sodium-reduced vegetable broth
1½ tsp	salt
½ tsp	pepper
1	bunch spinach, stemmed
1 cup	whipping cream (35%)
2 tbsp	lemon juice

How to make it

In Dutch oven or large heavy-bottomed saucepan, heat oil over medium-high heat; cook garlic, stirring, until fragrant, about 30 seconds. Add asparagus and peas; cook, stirring, until asparagus is tender-crisp, about 4 minutes.

Stir in broth, salt and pepper; bring to boil. Reduce heat simmer; cook, stirring occasionally, until asparagus and peas are tender, 3 to 5 minutes. Stir in spinach; cook until wilted, about 1 minute.

In blender, working in batches, purée soup until smooth. *(Make-ahead: Let cool slightly; refrigerate in airtight container for up to 2 days.)* Return soup to pan.

In bowl, beat cream until thickened. Stir half of the cream and the lemon juice into soup until no streaks remain. Ladle soup into serving bowls; spoon remaining cream over top.

TIP FROM THE TEST KITCHEN
Choose thick stalks of asparagus for the best flavour and texture, and purée the soup in batches for a silky-smooth finish.

NUTRITIONAL INFORMATION, PER SERVING: about 166 cal, 5 g pro, 12 g total fat (7 g sat. fat), 12 g carb (4 g dietary fibre, 4 g sugar), 38 mg chol, 733 mg sodium, 421 mg potassium. % RDI: 7% calcium, 13% iron, 39% vit A, 28% vit C, 67% folate.

Roasted Carrot and Parsnip Soup With Whipped Goat Cheese and Kale Chips

HANDS-ON TIME	•	TOTAL TIME	•	MAKES
30 MINUTES		1½ HOURS		10 SERVINGS

What you need

CARROT AND PARSNIP SOUP

8	carrots, chopped
4	parsnips, peeled and chopped
4	shallots, halved
3	cloves garlic
1 tbsp	olive oil
½ tsp	salt
1	pkg (900 mL) sodium-reduced chicken broth

KALE CHIPS

6 cups	torn stemmed kale
2 tsp	olive oil
¼ tsp	sweet paprika
pinch	salt

WHIPPED GOAT CHEESE

130 g	soft goat cheese
quarter	pkg (250 g pkg) cream cheese, softened
½ cup	whipping cream (35%)
1 tbsp	lemon juice
pinch	pepper

How to make it

CARROT AND PARSNIP SOUP: In roasting pan, toss together carrots, parsnips, shallots, garlic, oil and salt. Roast in 450°F (230°C) oven, stirring once, until softened and browned, about 1 hour.

Scrape into Dutch oven or large heavy-bottomed saucepan. Stir in broth and 1 cup water; bring to boil. Reduce heat to simmer; cook for 5 minutes. In blender or food processor, working in batches, purée mixture until smooth. *(Make-ahead: Refrigerate in airtight container for up to 3 days.)* Ladle into serving bowls.

KALE CHIPS: While soup is simmering, toss together kale, oil, paprika and salt; arrange in single layer on parchment paper–lined rimmed baking sheet. Bake in 350°F (180°C) oven until crisp and darkened, 12 to 15 minutes. *(Make-ahead: Store in airtight container for up to 8 hours.)* Serve over soup.

WHIPPED GOAT CHEESE: While kale is baking, in blender or food processor, whip together goat cheese, cream cheese, cream, lemon juice and pepper until smooth and light. *(Make-ahead: Refrigerate in airtight container for up to 2 days.)* Dollop over soup.

TIP FROM THE TEST KITCHEN

These kale chips make a great snack on their own. You can switch up the flavours by seasoning the kale with your favourite spices; chili powder, curry powder and garam masala are great options.

NUTRITIONAL INFORMATION, PER SERVING: about 292 cal, 8 g pro, 12 g total fat (6 g sat. fat), 42 g carb (9 g dietary fibre, 13 g sugar), 29 mg chol, 493 mg sodium, 969 mg potassium. % RDI: 13% calcium, 14% iron, 195% vit A, 58% vit C, 55% folate.

Slow Cooker Kale and Chorizo Soup

HANDS-ON TIME
20 MINUTES

•

TOTAL TIME
6½ HOURS

•

MAKES
6 TO 8 SERVINGS

What you need

225 g	dry-cured chorizo or chouriço, halved lengthwise and sliced crosswise
1	Spanish onion, sliced
4	cloves garlic, sliced
450 g	yellow-fleshed potatoes (about 3), peeled, halved lengthwise and sliced
2	bay leaves
1 tsp	sweet paprika
½ tsp	salt
¼ tsp	pepper
4 cups	sodium-reduced chicken broth
1	bunch kale, trimmed and shredded

How to make it

In skillet, cook chorizo over medium-high heat, stirring, until browned. Using slotted spoon, transfer to slow cooker. Drain any fat from pan (do not wipe clean).

In same skillet, cook onion and garlic over medium heat, stirring occasionally, until softened and light golden, about 8 minutes. Transfer to slow cooker.

Add potatoes, bay leaves, paprika, salt and pepper to slow cooker; stir in broth and 4 cups water. Cover and cook on low until potatoes are tender, 6 to 8 hours.

Discard bay leaves. Using slotted spoon, remove as much chorizo as possible to bowl; set aside.

Add kale to slow cooker; cover and cook on high until tender, about 10 minutes. Using immersion blender, purée soup until almost smooth with a few chunks. Stir in chorizo. *(Make-ahead: Refrigerate in airtight container for up to 3 days or freeze for up to 2 weeks.)*

TIP FROM THE TEST KITCHEN
This soup freezes well, but it may thicken as it stands; thin with water and adjust seasonings as needed when you reheat it.

NUTRITIONAL INFORMATION, PER EACH OF 8 SERVINGS:
about 213 cal, 11 g pro, 11 g total fat (4 g sat. fat), 18 g carb (2 g dietary fibre, 4 g sugar), 25 mg chol, 817 mg sodium, 515 mg potassium.
% RDI: 8% calcium, 11% iron, 60% vit A, 82% vit C, 10% folate.

Beet Borscht

HANDS-ON TIME	•	TOTAL TIME	•	MAKES
1 HOUR		1 HOUR		10 TO 12 SERVINGS

What you need

2 tbsp	vegetable oil
1	onion, diced
3	cloves garlic, minced
½ tsp	caraway seeds
675 g	red beets, peeled and diced
5 cups	diced green cabbage
280 g	white potatoes (about 2 small), cubed
2	ribs celery, diced
1	carrot, diced
2	bay leaves
1¾ tsp	salt
½ tsp	pepper
1	can (156 mL) tomato paste
1 tbsp	packed brown sugar
3 tbsp	vinegar

How to make it

In Dutch oven or large heavy-bottomed saucepan, heat oil over medium-high heat; cook onion, garlic and caraway seeds, stirring occasionally, until onion is softened and light golden, about 4 minutes.

Reduce heat to medium. Stir in beets, cabbage, potatoes, celery, carrot, bay leaves, salt and pepper; cook, stirring often, until beets are just starting to soften, about 10 minutes.

Stir in tomato paste and brown sugar; cook, stirring, for 2 minutes. Stir in 10 cups water; bring to boil. Reduce heat to simmer; cook, stirring occasionally, until vegetables are tender, about 40 minutes.

Discard bay leaves; stir in vinegar. *(Make-ahead: Refrigerate in airtight container for up to 3 days or freeze for up to 2 weeks.)*

TIP FROM THE TEST KITCHEN

This versatile borscht is delicious hot or cold. It's dairy-free and vegan, as long as you can resist the traditional dollop of sour cream (or plain Greek yogurt). Serve with a sprinkle of chopped fresh dill.

NUTRITIONAL INFORMATION, PER EACH OF 12 SERVINGS:
about 85 cal, 2 g pro, 2 g total fat (trace sat. fat), 12 g carb (3 g dietary fibre), 0 mg chol, 398 mg sodium, 425 mg potassium. % RDI: 3% calcium, 8% iron, 14% vit A, 23% vit C, 20% folate.

Rutabaga Soup With Chive-Basil Oil

HANDS-ON TIME	TOTAL TIME	MAKES
30 MINUTES	1 HOUR	6 TO 8 SERVINGS

What you need

RUTABAGA SOUP

1 tbsp	olive oil
2	large ribs celery, chopped
1	onion, chopped
1	carrot, chopped
4	cloves garlic, minced
1 tbsp	chopped fresh thyme
¼ tsp	ground ginger
pinch	nutmeg
1	rutabaga, peeled and cut in 1-inch (2.5 cm) chunks (about 4 cups)
2	large yellow-fleshed potatoes, peeled and cubed
1	pkg (900 mL) no-salt-added vegetable broth
⅓ cup	whipping cream (35%)
1½ tsp	Dijon mustard
1½ tsp	salt
½ tsp	pepper

CHIVE-BASIL OIL

½ cup	coarsely chopped fresh chives
½ cup	lightly packed fresh basil leaves
½ cup	olive oil

GARNISH

3 tbsp	sour cream
¼ cup	sliced natural (skin-on) almonds, toasted

How to make it

RUTABAGA SOUP: In Dutch oven or large heavy-bottomed saucepan, heat oil over medium heat; cook celery, onion and carrot, stirring occasionally, until softened, about 5 minutes. Add garlic, thyme, ginger and nutmeg; cook, stirring, until fragrant, about 1 minute.

Stir in rutabaga, potatoes, broth and 2 cups water; bring to boil. Reduce heat to simmer; cover and cook until rutabaga and potatoes are tender, 20 to 25 minutes. Let cool for 10 minutes.

In blender, purée soup, in batches, until smooth. Return to clean Dutch oven. Add cream, mustard, salt and pepper; cook over medium heat, stirring, until hot, about 4 minutes. Ladle into serving bowls.

CHIVE-BASIL OIL: While soup is simmering, in small saucepan of boiling water, cook chives and basil for 1 minute; drain. Transfer to bowl of ice water to chill; drain. Using hands, squeeze out liquid; pat dry.

In food processor, pulse chive mixture into coarse paste. With motor running, add oil in thin steady stream, scraping down side twice, until smooth, about 4 minutes. *(Make-ahead: Refrigerate in airtight container for up to 3 days; bring to room temperature before serving.)* Drizzle 1 tsp of the oil over each bowl of soup.

GARNISH: Spoon sour cream onto soup. Sprinkle with almonds.

NUTRITIONAL INFORMATION, PER EACH OF 8 SERVINGS:
about 306 cal, 11 g pro, 21 g total fat (5 g sat. fat), 27 g carb (3 g dietary fibre, 8 g sugar), 15 mg chol, 501 mg sodium, 637 mg potassium. % RDI: 8% calcium, 9% iron, 27% vit A, 37% vit C, 13% folate.

Slow Cooker Chicken Tikka Masala

HANDS-ON TIME	•	TOTAL TIME	•	MAKES
15 MINUTES		8½ HOURS		8 SERVINGS

What you need

How to make it

CHICKEN TIKKA MASALA

1	can (796 mL) diced tomatoes
1½ cups	sliced sweet onion (about 1 small)
1	can (156 mL) tomato paste
2 tbsp	packed brown sugar
1 tbsp	finely chopped peeled fresh ginger
3	cloves garlic, finely chopped
2 tsp	each ground cumin and garam masala
1 tsp	paprika
½ tsp	each salt and turmeric
pinch	cayenne pepper
900 g	boneless skinless chicken breasts, cut in 1-inch (2.5 cm) chunks
¼ cup	whipping cream (35%)
1 tbsp	lemon juice

CUCUMBER RAITA

1 cup	grated peeled cucumber (about half cucumber)
pinch	salt
1 cup	plain Balkan-style yogurt
¼ cup	chopped fresh cilantro
2 tsp	lemon juice

CHICKEN TIKKA MASALA: In slow cooker, combine tomatoes, onion, tomato paste, brown sugar, ginger, garlic, cumin, garam masala, paprika, salt, turmeric, cayenne pepper and ⅔ cup water. Cover and cook on low for 8 to 10 hours.

Using immersion blender, purée tomato mixture until smooth. Add chicken; cover and cook on high until chicken is no longer pink inside, about 30 minutes. Stir in cream and lemon juice. *(Make-ahead: Cover and refrigerate for up to 24 hours. Reheat before serving.)*

CUCUMBER RAITA: While chicken is cooking, in colander, sprinkle cucumber with salt; let stand for 5 minutes. Squeeze out excess liquid and pat dry.

In small bowl, stir together cucumber, yogurt, cilantro and lemon juice. *(Make-ahead: Cover and refrigerate for up to 24 hours.)* Serve with Chicken Tikka Masala.

TIP FROM THE TEST KITCHEN

Garam masala is a potent spice blend that usually includes cardamom, cinnamon, nutmeg, coriander, mace and cloves. To save prep time, look for the ready-made mix in the spice section of the grocery store.

NUTRITIONAL INFORMATION, PER SERVING: about 239 cal, 29 g pro, 7 g total fat (3 g sat. fat), 17 g carb (3 g dietary fibre, 10 g sugar), 80 mg chol, 379 mg sodium, 882 mg potassium. % RDI: 10% calcium, 21% iron, 11% vit A, 37% vit C, 8% folate.

Beef and Mushrooms With Gravy

HANDS-ON TIME	•	TOTAL TIME	•	MAKES
1 HOUR		3 HOURS		8 SERVINGS

What you need

2 cups	boiling water
2	pkg (each 14 g) dried mixed exotic mushrooms, chopped
¼ cup	butter
2	sweet onions, thinly sliced
4	cloves garlic, minced
900 g	beef stewing cubes
¾ tsp	each salt and pepper
⅔ cup	all-purpose flour
2 tbsp	vegetable oil
1	pkg (900 mL) sodium-reduced beef broth
½ tsp	dried thyme
2	bay leaves
2 tsp	Dijon mustard
1 tsp	Worcestershire sauce
2	pkg (each 227 g) cremini mushrooms, thinly sliced

How to make it

In bowl, pour boiling water over dried mushrooms; set aside. In Dutch oven or large heavy-bottomed saucepan, melt 2 tbsp of the butter over medium heat; cook onions, stirring occasionally, until golden, about 25 minutes. Add garlic; cook, stirring, for 1 minute. Scrape into separate bowl; set aside.

Toss beef with half each of the salt and pepper; toss in 3 tbsp of the flour. In same pan, heat oil over medium-high heat; working in batches, cook beef, stirring, until browned, about 7 minutes. Stir in onion mixture, 3 cups of the broth, the thyme, bay leaves, soaked mushrooms and soaking liquid, remaining salt and pepper and 2 cups water. Bring to boil; reduce heat to simmer; cover and cook just until beef is tender, about 1½ hours. Discard bay leaves; stir in mustard and Worcestershire sauce.

While beef mixture is simmering, in skillet, melt remaining butter over medium-high heat; cook cremini mushrooms, stirring occasionally, until softened, about 5 minutes. Add remaining flour; cook, stirring occasionally, until flour is golden, about 3 minutes. Whisk in remaining broth. Stir into stew; bring to boil. Reduce heat to simmer; cook, stirring occasionally, until thickened, about 20 minutes. (*Make-ahead: Let cool. Refrigerate in airtight container for up to 3 days or freeze for up to 1 month.*)

TIP FROM THE TEST KITCHEN

Spoon this rich stew over mashed potatoes for a satisfying comfort-food dinner. Or serve it with baked potato wedges and top with fresh cheese curds for a decadent homemade poutine.

NUTRITIONAL INFORMATION, PER SERVING: about 377 cal, 28 g pro, 21 g total fat (9 g sat. fat), 20 g carb (3 g dietary fibre, 6 g sugar), 82 mg chol, 658 mg sodium, 734 mg potassium. % RDI: 5% calcium, 25% iron, 5% vit A, 7% vit C, 21% folate.

Sweet and Sour Beef Stew With Prunes and Apricots

HANDS-ON TIME	·	TOTAL TIME	·	MAKES
35 MINUTES		3 HOURS		10 SERVINGS

What you need

1 tbsp	vegetable oil
2	onions, thinly sliced
2	ribs celery, thinly sliced
1.35 kg	beef stewing cubes
½ tsp	each salt and pepper
2	cloves garlic, minced
2 tsp	ground ginger
½ tsp	each cinnamon and ground allspice
2	bay leaves
3 cups	sodium-reduced beef broth
1 cup	dry red wine
⅓ cup	cider vinegar
2 tbsp	packed brown sugar
2 tsp	Worcestershire sauce
4	carrots, chopped
2	white turnips, peeled and cubed
½ cup	pitted prunes, chopped
½ cup	dried apricots, chopped
2 tbsp	all-purpose flour

How to make it

In Dutch oven or large heavy-bottomed saucepan, heat 1 tsp of the oil over medium heat; cook onions and celery, stirring occasionally, until softened, about 7 minutes. Scrape into bowl.

Toss together beef, salt and pepper. Add remaining oil to pan; heat over medium-high heat. Working in batches, cook beef, stirring occasionally, until browned, about 6 minutes. Add garlic; cook, stirring, until fragrant, about 1 minute.

Add onion mixture, ginger, cinnamon, allspice and bay leaves; cook, stirring, for 1 minute. Stir in broth, wine, vinegar, brown sugar and Worcestershire sauce; bring to boil. Reduce heat to simmer; cover and cook for 1½ hours.

Stir in carrots, turnips, prunes and apricots; cook, stirring occasionally, until turnips are tender, about 45 minutes. Discard bay leaves.

Whisk flour with 2 tbsp water; whisk into stew. Simmer until slightly thickened, about 10 minutes. *(Make-ahead: Let cool for 30 minutes. Refrigerate in airtight container for up to 3 days or freeze for up to 1 month.)*

TIP FROM THE TEST KITCHEN
Serve this luxurious stew with a side of couscous for a Moroccan-style meal.

NUTRITIONAL INFORMATION, PER SERVING: about 341 cal, 29 g pro, 15 g total fat (6 g sat. fat), 22 g carb (3 g dietary fibre, 13 g sugar), 80 mg chol, 452 mg sodium, 778 mg potassium. % RDI: 6% calcium, 26% iron, 54% vit A, 13% vit C, 10% folate.

Speedy Mini Lasagnas

cover

HANDS-ON TIME	•	TOTAL TIME	•	MAKES
20 MINUTES		30 MINUTES		4 SERVINGS

What you need | How to make it

8	lasagna noodles, broken in bite-size pieces
2 tsp	olive oil
300 g	extra-lean ground beef
1	onion, diced
3	cloves garlic, finely grated or pressed
1 tbsp	Italian herb seasoning
½ tsp	salt
¼ tsp	pepper
1	small zucchini (peel-on), grated
1	bottle (680 mL) strained tomatoes (passata)
4 tsp	liquid honey
⅔ cup	extra-smooth ricotta cheese
½ cup	grated Parmesan cheese
½ cup	chopped fresh basil
1	egg yolk
½ cup	shredded mozzarella cheese

In large saucepan of boiling lightly salted water, cook noodles according to package instructions until al dente. Drain and set aside.

Meanwhile, in large skillet, heat oil over medium-high heat; cook beef, onion, two-thirds of the garlic, the Italian seasoning, salt and pepper, stirring occasionally and breaking up beef with spoon, until beef is no longer pink and onion is softened, about 5 minutes.

Add zucchini; cook, stirring, until softened, about 2 minutes. Reduce heat to medium. Add strained tomatoes and honey; cook, stirring, until hot and combined, about 1 minute. Stir in noodles. Spoon into four 1½-cup (375 mL) ramekins.

In bowl, stir together ricotta, Parmesan, basil, egg yolk and remaining garlic until smooth. Spoon over noodle mixture, spreading to edges of ramekins. Sprinkle with mozzarella. *(Make-ahead: Let cool; cover with foil and refrigerate for up to 24 hours. Reheat on rimmed baking sheet in 325°F/160°C oven until heated through, about 30 minutes, before continuing with recipe.)*

Broil on rimmed baking sheet on centre rack until tops are browned and bubbly, 3 to 4 minutes. Let stand for 5 minutes before serving.

TIP FROM THE TEST KITCHEN
Broiling the lasagnas on the centre rack allows the ricotta mixture to become hot and bubbly without overbrowning the tops.

NUTRITIONAL INFORMATION, PER SERVING: about 587 cal, 38 g pro, 22 g total fat (11 g sat. fat), 57 g carb (5 g dietary fibre, 12 g sugar), 125 mg chol, 827 mg sodium, 495 mg potassium. % RDI: 32% calcium, 36% iron, 53% vit A, 12% vit C, 63% folate.

Fresh Tomato Sauce

HANDS-ON TIME	TOTAL TIME	MAKES
30 MINUTES	2 HOURS	ABOUT 11 CUPS

What you need

4 kg	plum tomatoes (about 40)
2	onions, chopped
½ cup	olive oil
3	cloves garlic, minced
1	can (156 mL) tomato paste
1¼ tsp	salt
½ tsp	pepper

How to make it

Score an X in bottom of each tomato. In large saucepan of boiling water, cook tomatoes until skins begin to loosen, about 1 minute. Using slotted spoon, transfer to bowl of ice water and chill for 20 seconds; drain.

Working over fine-mesh sieve set over bowl, peel off tomato skins; discard. Core tomatoes and remove seeds to sieve; press seeds to extract juice, reserving 3 cups juice. (Reserve remaining tomato juice for another use.) Set juice aside. Discard seeds and cores.

In food processor, working in batches, purée tomato flesh until smooth. (Purée should yield approximately 10 cups.) Scrape into bowl. Set aside. In food processor, purée onions until smooth.

In Dutch oven or large heavy-bottomed saucepan, heat oil over medium heat; cook onions, stirring occasionally, until golden and liquid has evaporated, about 12 minutes. Add garlic; cook, stirring, until fragrant, about 1 minute. Stir in puréed tomatoes, reserved tomato juice, tomato paste, salt and pepper. Bring to boil; reduce heat to simmer, uncover and cook, stirring occasionally, until sauce has reduced to about 11 cups, about 1½ hours. *(Make-ahead: Let cool; refrigerate in airtight container for up to 1 week or freeze for up to 2 months.)*

VARIATION

Pressure Cooker Fresh Tomato Sauce

Follow first 3 paragraphs as directed. In pressure cooker, heat oil over medium heat; cook onions and garlic as directed. Stir in puréed tomatoes, 2 cups of the reserved tomato juice, the tomato paste, salt and pepper. (Reserve remaining tomato juice for another use.) Secure lid; bring to high pressure over high heat. Reduce heat while maintaining high pressure; cook for 20 minutes. Remove from heat; let pressure release completely, about 2 minutes.

NUTRITIONAL INFORMATION, PER ½ CUP: about 80 cal, 2 g pro, 5 g total fat (1 g sat. fat), 8 g carb (2 g dietary fibre, 5 g sugar), 0 mg chol, 146 mg sodium, 429 mg potassium. % RDI: 2% calcium, 5% iron, 12% vit A, 32% vit C, 8% folate.

Smoky Pork Bolognese Sauce

HANDS-ON TIME
15 MINUTES

•

TOTAL TIME
1½ HOURS

•

MAKES
ABOUT 7 CUPS

What you need

450 g	lean ground pork
2	strips bacon, chopped
2	carrots, diced
2	ribs celery, diced
1	onion, diced
3	cloves garlic, minced
4 cups	Fresh Tomato Sauce (see recipe, page 43) or good-quality plain tomato sauce
1 cup	dry red wine
1 tsp	granulated sugar
1 tsp	dried oregano
¼ tsp	hot pepper flakes
1	bay leaf
¼ cup	chopped fresh parsley

How to make it

In Dutch oven or large heavy-bottomed saucepan, cook pork and bacon over medium-high heat, breaking up pork with spoon, until no longer pink, about 7 minutes. Using slotted spoon, remove mixture to bowl. Set aside. Drain all but 2 tbsp fat from Dutch oven.

Add carrots, celery and onion to Dutch oven. Reduce heat to medium and cook, stirring occasionally, until softened, about 10 minutes. Add garlic; cook, stirring, until fragrant, about 1 minute.

Stir in pork mixture, tomato sauce, wine, sugar, oregano, hot pepper flakes and bay leaf. Bring to boil; reduce heat to simmer, cover and cook, stirring occasionally, until slightly thickened, about 1 hour. Discard bay leaf. Stir in parsley. *(Make-ahead: Let cool; refrigerate in airtight container for up to 2 days or freeze for up to 2 months.)*

TIP FROM THE TEST KITCHEN

Freeze this sauce in meal-size portions for an easy dinner solution on busy weeknights; just reheat and serve over hot pasta, such as rotini or rigatoni—two shapes that hold hearty sauces well.

NUTRITIONAL INFORMATION, PER ½ CUP: about 135 cal, 8 g pro, 8 g total fat (2 g sat. fat), 8 g carb (2 g dietary fibre, 4 g sugar), 22 mg chol, 148 mg sodium, 433 mg potassium. % RDI: 3% calcium, 7% iron, 27% vit A, 23% vit C, 8% folate.

Slow Cooker Tomato and Sausage Pasta

HANDS-ON TIME	•	TOTAL TIME	•	MAKES
20 MINUTES		6½ HOURS		8 SERVINGS

What you need

4	mild Italian sausages (about 400 g total), casings removed and broken in bite-size pieces
1	onion, sliced
1	eggplant, cut in ¾-inch (2 cm) pieces
1	pkg (227 g) cremini mushrooms, sliced
3	cloves garlic, sliced
1	bottle (680 mL) strained tomatoes (passata)
2 tbsp	tomato paste
2 tsp	balsamic vinegar
1 tsp	Italian herb seasoning
¼ tsp	hot pepper flakes
pinch	each salt and pepper
1 tbsp	all-purpose flour
700 g	fusilli
½ cup	grated Parmesan cheese
¼ cup	fresh basil leaves, torn

How to make it

In slow cooker, combine sausages, onion, eggplant, mushrooms and garlic; stir in strained tomatoes, tomato paste, vinegar, Italian seasoning, hot pepper flakes, salt and pepper. Cover and cook on low until sausage is cooked through and eggplant is tender, 6 to 8 hours.

Whisk flour with 1 tbsp water until smooth; whisk into slow cooker. Cover and cook on high until slightly thickened, about 10 minutes. (*Make-ahead: Let cool for 30 minutes. Refrigerate in airtight container for up to 3 days.*)

Meanwhile, in large saucepan of boiling salted water, cook pasta according to package instructions until al dente; drain. To serve, spoon sauce over pasta; top with Parmesan and basil.

TIP FROM THE TEST KITCHEN
Button, cremini and portobello mushrooms are all strains of the same species. Button and cremini mushrooms can easily be substituted with each other. Portobellos have a firmer texture and bolder flavour.

NUTRITIONAL INFORMATION, PER SERVING: about 535 cal, 22 g pro, 14 g total fat (5 g sat. fat), 79 g carb (5 g dietary fibre, 8 g sugar), 27 mg chol, 818 mg sodium, 630 mg potassium. % RDI: 11% calcium, 38% iron, 3% vit A, 8% vit C, 99% folate.

The Ultimate Beef Burger

HANDS-ON TIME	•	TOTAL TIME	•	MAKES
20 MINUTES		25 MINUTES		6 BURGERS

What you need

1 cup	fresh bread crumbs
⅔ cup	sodium-reduced beef broth
450 g	medium ground beef
450 g	ground sirloin
½ tsp	salt
¼ tsp	pepper
6	buns (hamburger, pretzel or pain au lait), split and toasted

How to make it

In bowl, mix bread crumbs with broth; let stand for 5 minutes.

In large baking dish, add beef and sirloin; sprinkle with bread crumb mixture, salt and pepper. Mix gently just until combined and no streaks of bread crumb mixture are visible (do not overmix).

Shape into six 5- x ½-inch (12 x 1 cm) patties. *(Make-ahead: Layer between parchment paper in airtight container; refrigerate for up to 24 hours.)*

Place on greased grill over medium-high heat; close lid and grill, turning once, until instant-read thermometer inserted sideways into patties reads 160°F (71°C), about 8 minutes. (Alternatively, in grill pan or skillet, heat up to 2 tsp olive oil over medium-high heat and cook patties, turning once.) Serve in buns.

VARIATION
The Ultimate Pub-Style Burger
Shape beef mixture into six 3½- x 1-inch (9 x 2.5 cm) patties. Place on greased grill over medium-high heat; close lid and grill for 7 minutes. Turn patties and reduce heat to medium; close lid and grill until instant-read thermometer inserted sideways into patties reads 160°F (71°C), about 7 minutes. (Use smaller buns for these thicker patties.)

NUTRITIONAL INFORMATION, PER BURGER: about 416 cal, 34 g pro, 18 g total fat (7 g sat. fat), 28 g carb (1 g dietary fibre, 4 g sugar), 80 mg chol, 611 mg sodium, 388 mg potassium. % RDI: 8% calcium, 34% iron, 27% folate.

Chef's Salad Wrap

HANDS-ON TIME	•	TOTAL TIME	•	MAKES
15 MINUTES		20 MINUTES		4 SERVINGS

What you need

4	eggs
2 tbsp	extra-virgin olive oil
1 tbsp	red wine vinegar
1 tsp	Dijon mustard
4 cups	loosely packed chopped romaine lettuce
¾ cup	chopped cucumber
3	radishes, thinly sliced
1 tbsp	chopped fresh chives
4	slices Cheddar cheese (about 85 g total)
4	large flour tortillas (10 inches/25 cm)
4	thin slices Black Forest ham (about 55 g total)

How to make it

In saucepan, cover eggs with 1 inch (2.5 cm) water. Bring to boil; cook for 1 minute. Remove from heat; cover and let stand for 12 minutes. Drain eggs and run under cold water until cool, about 2 minutes; drain again. *(Make-ahead: Refrigerate for up to 48 hours.)* Peel and slice.

Meanwhile, in bowl, whisk together oil, vinegar and mustard; stir in lettuce, cucumber, radishes and chives.

Place 1 slice Cheddar on centre of each tortilla; top with 1 slice ham and one-quarter of the egg slices. Mound lettuce mixture on top; roll up. *(Make-ahead: Wrap tightly in plastic wrap or foil and refrigerate for up to 12 hours.)*

VARIATION
Chicken Swiss Salad Wrap
Substitute sliced deli chicken for the ham, and Swiss cheese for the Cheddar.

TIP FROM THE TEST KITCHEN
For an extra boost of fibre, use whole-wheat tortillas.

NUTRITIONAL INFORMATION, PER SERVING: about 427 cal, 20 g pro, 24 g total fat (8 g sat. fat), 35 g carb (2 g dietary fibre, 2 g sugar), 212 mg chol, 814 mg sodium, 289 mg potassium. % RDI: 20% calcium, 26% iron, 57% vit A, 22% vit C, 45% folate.

Tahini Falafel Burgers With Cucumber Salsa

HANDS-ON TIME
20 MINUTES

•

TOTAL TIME
20 MINUTES

•

MAKES
4 SERVINGS

What you need

How to make it

FALAFEL BURGERS

2	green onions, chopped
3	cloves garlic, chopped
1	can (540 mL) chickpeas, drained and rinsed
¼ cup	chopped fresh cilantro
1	egg
1 tsp	each ground cumin and chili powder
¼ tsp	each salt and pepper
¼ cup	chickpea flour or all-purpose flour
4 tsp	vegetable oil
4	large green or red lettuce leaves, separated
4 tsp	tahini

CUCUMBER SALSA

2	plum tomatoes, seeded and diced
1 cup	diced seeded English cucumber (about half cucumber)
1 tbsp	chopped fresh mint
2 tsp	white wine vinegar
pinch	each salt and pepper

FALAFEL BURGERS: In food processor, pulse green onions with garlic until finely chopped. Add chickpeas, cilantro, egg, cumin, chili powder, salt and pepper; pulse into fine paste. Add chickpea flour; pulse until combined. Shape into 4 balls; flatten each to ¾-inch (2 cm) thick patties. *(Make-ahead: Layer between parchment paper in airtight container; refrigerate for up to 24 hours.)*

In large nonstick skillet, heat oil over medium heat; cook patties, turning once, until golden, 6 to 8 minutes. Arrange 1 patty in each lettuce leaf; drizzle with tahini.

CUCUMBER SALSA: While patties are cooking, in bowl, stir together tomatoes, cucumber, mint, vinegar, salt and pepper. Serve over falafel.

TIP FROM THE TEST KITCHEN
Serving these falafel burgers in lettuce leaves makes them extra-light, but if you don't mind the extra carbs, use pitas or hamburger buns. Mixed sprouts, thinly sliced onions and pickled turnip are all great topping options.

NUTRITIONAL INFORMATION, PER SERVING: about 242 cal, 10 g pro, 11 g total fat (1 g sat. fat), 27 g carb (7 g dietary fibre, 6 g sugar), 48 mg chol, 348 mg sodium, 374 mg potassium. % RDI: 9% calcium, 20% iron, 17% vit A, 12% vit C, 35% folate.

Mini Cubanos

HANDS-ON TIME	•	TOTAL TIME	•	MAKES
50 MINUTES		5 HOURS		24 PIECES

What you need | How to make it

MARINATED PORK TENDERLOIN

⅓ cup	finely chopped onion
¼ cup	each orange juice and olive oil
1 tbsp	each lemon juice and lime juice
1	clove garlic, minced
¼ tsp	each salt and dried oregano
450 g	pork tenderloin, trimmed

SANDWICHES

¼ cup	butter, softened
12	slices ½-inch (1 cm) thick French or Italian bread
2 tbsp	yellow mustard (optional)
12	slices Swiss cheese
6	slices Black Forest ham
12	slices dill pickle

MARINATED PORK TENDERLOIN: In shallow baking dish or resealable bag, stir together onion, orange juice, oil, lemon juice, lime juice, garlic, salt and oregano. Add pork, turning to coat. Cover and refrigerate for 4 hours. *(Make-ahead: Refrigerate for up to 24 hours.)*

Place pork on greased grill over medium-high heat. Close lid and grill, turning occasionally, until juices run clear when pork is pierced and just a hint of pink remains inside, 20 to 25 minutes. Cover loosely with foil; let stand for 10 minutes. *(Make-ahead: Cover and refrigerate for up to 24 hours. Reheat pork if desired.)* Cut into ¼-inch (5 mm) thick slices; set aside.

SANDWICHES: Spread butter on 1 side of each bread slice. Spread mustard (if using) on other side of each bread slice. Arrange half of the bread slices, buttered side down, on work surface; top each with 1 slice Swiss, 1 slice ham, 2 slices pickle, one-sixth of the pork and another slice of Swiss. Top with remaining bread slices, buttered side up.

Using panini press, grill sandwiches until Swiss is melted, about 10 minutes (or cook in greased skillet over medium heat, turning once). Cut each sandwich into quarters.

TIP FROM THE TEST KITCHEN

Before marinating the tenderloin, don't forget to slice off any silverskin (the thin, shiny layer of connective tissue on the surface). Sometimes the butcher has already removed it for you, but often it's still on the tenderloin at the time of sale.

NUTRITIONAL INFORMATION, PER PIECE: about 116 cal, 9 g pro, 6 g total fat (3 g sat. fat), 7 g carb, (trace dietary fibre), 27 mg chol, 203 mg sodium, 100 mg potassium. % RDI: 8% calcium, 4% iron, 4% vit A, 5% folate

Spice-Rubbed Flank Steak

HANDS-ON TIME	•	TOTAL TIME	•	MAKES
20 MINUTES		4½ HOURS		12 TO 16 SERVINGS

What you need

4	cloves garlic, finely grated or pressed
4 tsp	grated fresh ginger
4 tsp	olive oil
2 tsp	each ground coriander, ground cumin and dry mustard
1 tsp	salt
2	beef flank marinating steaks (each about 650 g)

How to make it

In small bowl, stir together garlic, ginger, oil, coriander, cumin, mustard and salt. Set aside.

Using fork, prick steaks all over on both sides. Rub garlic mixture all over steaks. Place in large resealable plastic bag; seal bag and refrigerate for 4 hours. *(Make-ahead: Refrigerate for up to 24 hours.)*

Place steaks on greased grill over medium-high heat; grill, uncovered, turning at least twice, until instant-read thermometer inserted in centres reads 140°F (60°C), 10 to 12 minutes. Remove to rack and let rest, uncovered, for 5 minutes or until instant-read thermometer inserted in centres reads 145°F (63°C) for medium-rare. *(Make-ahead: Refrigerate in airtight container for up to 24 hours.)* Thinly slice across the grain.

TIP FROM THE TEST KITCHEN

Flank steaks are large, relatively thin cuts that cook quickly on the grill. Each steak serves six to eight people. Use leftovers for tasty steak sandwiches: pile sliced steak, grilled vegetables and mayo on crusty rolls.

NUTRITIONAL INFORMATION, PER EACH OF 16 SERVINGS:
about 145 cal, 19 g pro, 7 g total fat (3 g sat. fat), 1 g carb (trace dietary fibre, trace sugar), 39 mg chol, 178 mg sodium, 194 mg potassium. % RDI: 1% calcium, 14% iron, 2% folate.

Rosemary-Rubbed Beef Brisket

HANDS-ON TIME	•	TOTAL TIME	•	MAKES
30 MINUTES		5½ HOURS		10 TO 12 SERVINGS

What you need

6	cloves garlic, minced
3 tbsp	fresh rosemary leaves, minced
3 tbsp	olive oil
2 tbsp	Dijon mustard
½ tsp	each onion powder and pepper
1.8 kg	boneless beef brisket pot roast
¼ tsp	kosher salt
2 cups	dry red wine
2 cups	sodium-reduced beef broth
2 tbsp	cornstarch

How to make it

Stir together garlic, rosemary, 2 tbsp of the oil, the mustard, onion powder and pepper; rub all over beef. Cover and refrigerate for 2 hours. *(Make-ahead: Refrigerate for up to 24 hours.)*

Sprinkle beef with salt. In large skillet, heat remaining oil over medium-high heat; brown beef all over. Transfer to large roasting pan.

Stir wine with broth; pour into pan. Cover and braise in 325°F (160°C) oven until fork-tender, 3 to 4 hours. Transfer to cutting board and cover loosely with foil; let stand for 10 minutes before thinly slicing across the grain (if making ahead, don't slice it yet).

Meanwhile, strain pan juices through fine-mesh sieve; skim off fat. Return juices to pan and bring to boil. Whisk cornstarch with 2 tbsp water; whisk into pan and cook, whisking, until slightly thickened, about 1 minute. Serve with brisket. *(Make-ahead: Let brisket and sauce cool for 30 minutes. Return brisket to sauce; cover and refrigerate for up to 24 hours. Thinly slice across the grain; arrange in sauce. Cover and reheat in 325°F/160°C oven for about 1 hour.)*

TIP FROM THE TEST KITCHEN
If your brisket has the fat attached (which is ideal for maximum moistness), place it fat side up in the roasting pan.

NUTRITIONAL INFORMATION, PER EACH OF 12 SERVINGS:
about 381 cal, 28 g pro, 28 g total fat (10 g sat. fat), 3 g carb (trace dietary fibre, trace sugar), 97 mg chol, 271 mg sodium, 470 mg potassium. % RDI: 2% calcium, 20% iron, 3% folate.

Slow Cooker Creamy Tomato Pot Roast

HANDS-ON TIME	•	TOTAL TIME	•	MAKES
15 MINUTES		8½ HOURS		6 SERVINGS

What you need

1	large sweet onion, thinly sliced
1½ cups	sodium-reduced beef broth
½ cup	dry white wine
¼ cup	tomato paste
6	sprigs fresh thyme
2 tsp	garlic powder
¾ tsp	salt
¼ tsp	pepper
950 g	boneless beef blade pot roast, trimmed
¼ cup	whipping cream (35%)
3 tbsp	all-purpose flour
2 tbsp	chopped fresh parsley (optional)

How to make it

In slow cooker, combine onion, broth, wine, tomato paste, thyme, garlic powder, salt and pepper. Add beef, pushing to submerge. Cover and cook on low until beef is tender, 8 to 10 hours.

Using 2 slotted spoons, transfer beef to platter; remove any twine. Cover loosely with foil to keep warm. Skim fat from surface of cooking liquid; discard thyme.

Whisk cream with flour; gradually whisk into slow cooker. Cover and cook on high until thickened, about 15 minutes. Spoon onto beef. Sprinkle with parsley (if using). *(Make-ahead: Cover and refrigerate for up to 3 days.)*

TIP FROM THE TEST KITCHEN
You can freeze any leftover sauce in an airtight container for up to three weeks; serve it with meatloaf or use it in shepherd's pie.

NUTRITIONAL INFORMATION, PER SERVING: about 341 cal, 30 g pro, 20 g total fat (9 g sat. fat), 10 g carb (1 g dietary fibre, 4 g sugar), 97 mg chol, 555 mg sodium, 446 mg potassium. % RDI: 4% calcium, 26% iron, 5% vit A, 8% vit C, 10% folate.

Slow Cooker Pulled Beef Tacos

HANDS-ON TIME 20 MINUTES	•	**TOTAL TIME** 8½ HOURS	•	**MAKES** 16 TACOS

What you need

1	can (796 mL) diced tomatoes
1	can (156 mL) tomato paste
1	sweet onion, diced
1	jalapeño pepper, seeded and finely chopped
2 tsp	each ground cumin and garlic powder
1½ tsp	dried oregano
½ tsp	salt
¼ tsp	pepper
1.2 kg	boneless beef blade pot roast, trimmed
16	soft corn or flour tortillas (6 inches/15 cm), warmed

How to make it

In slow cooker, combine tomatoes, tomato paste, onion, jalapeño pepper, cumin, garlic powder, oregano, salt and pepper. Add beef, turning to coat. Cover and cook on low until beef is tender, 8 to 10 hours.

Using 2 slotted spoons, transfer beef to cutting board; remove any twine. Using 2 forks, shred into bite-size pieces. Transfer to bowl.

Skim fat from surface of cooking liquid. Add 2 cups of the cooking liquid to beef; toss to coat. *(Make-ahead: Cover and refrigerate for up to 3 days.)* Serve over tortillas.

TIP FROM THE TEST KITCHEN
You'll have extra sauce in the slow cooker. If you don't mind messy tacos, pour a little over top of each. Save any leftover sauce in your fridge or freezer—it makes a great base for chili.

NUTRITIONAL INFORMATION, PER TACO: about 159 cal, 15 g pro, 6 g total fat (2 g sat. fat), 10 g carb (2 g dietary fibre, 1 g sugar), 38 mg chol, 84 mg sodium, 214 mg potassium. % RDI: 3% calcium, 14% iron, 1% vit A, 5% vit C, 3% folate.

Mini Shepherd's Pies

HANDS-ON TIME
35 MINUTES

•

TOTAL TIME
1 HOUR

•

MAKES
4 SERVINGS

What you need

1	small onion, quartered
half	pkg (227 g cremini mushrooms
2	cloves garlic
450 g	extra-lean ground beef
1 tsp	olive oil
½ tsp	dried rosemary
1 tbsp	all-purpose flour
¼ cup	each frozen corn and frozen peas
1 tsp	Worcestershire sauce
½ tsp	each salt and pepper
675 g	yellow-fleshed potatoes, peeled and cut in 1-inch (2.5 cm) chunks
2 tbsp	butter
2	green onions, sliced

How to make it

In food processor, pulse together onion, mushrooms and garlic until finely chopped. Set aside.

In large nonstick skillet, cook beef over medium-high heat, breaking up with spoon, until no longer pink, about 8 minutes. Scrape into bowl. In same skillet, heat oil over medium-high heat; sauté onion mixture and rosemary until no liquid remains, about 4 minutes. Sprinkle with flour; cook, stirring often, for 2 minutes. Stir in corn, peas, Worcestershire sauce, half each of the salt and pepper and 1 cup water. Add beef and any juices; bring to boil. Reduce heat to simmer; cook, stirring, until thickened, about 2 minutes. Divide among four 1½-cup (375 mL) ramekins.

Meanwhile, in large saucepan of boiling lightly salted water, cook potatoes until tender, about 12 minutes. Reserving ½ cup of the cooking liquid, drain. Return potatoes to saucepan. Mash with half of the butter and the remaining salt and pepper, adding reserved cooking liquid, as needed, until smooth. Stir in green onions. Spoon over beef mixture, spreading to rims of ramekins. *(Make-ahead: Cover and refrigerate for up to 2 days; add 20 minutes to bake time.)* Dot tops with remaining butter. Bake on rimmed baking sheet in 400°F (200°C) oven until tops are golden, about 30 minutes.

NUTRITIONAL INFORMATION, PER SERVING: about 401 cal, 28 g pro, 16 g total fat (7 g sat. fat), 37 g carb (4 g dietary fibre, 4 g sugar), 77 mg chol, 804 mg sodium, 1,022 mg potassium. % RDI: 4% calcium, 24% iron, 8% vit A, 25% vit C, 17% folate.

Cheese and Jalapeño-Stuffed Chicken Thighs

HANDS-ON TIME	TOTAL TIME	MAKES
10 MINUTES	30 MINUTES	4 SERVINGS

What you need

1 cup	shredded old Cheddar cheese
⅓ cup	cream cheese, softened
2 tbsp	minced pickled jalapeño peppers
600 g	boneless skinless chicken thighs (about 8)
1 tbsp	olive oil
1 cup	panko bread crumbs

How to make it

In small bowl, stir together Cheddar, cream cheese and jalapeños; set aside.

Between waxed paper, pound chicken thighs to ¼-inch (5 mm) thickness. Drop Cheddar mixture by scant 1 tbsp onto centre of each thigh. Roll up, tucking in sides, and secure each with 2 toothpicks. *(Make-ahead: Refrigerate in airtight container for up to 24 hours.)* Brush chicken all over with oil. Add panko to small bowl; press all sides of chicken firmly into panko to coat. Place, seam side down, on parchment paper–lined rimmed baking sheet. Bake in 450°F (230°C) oven until golden and instant-read thermometer inserted into thickest part of each thigh 160°F (71°C), 20 to 25 minutes.

NUTRITIONAL INFORMATION, PER SERVING: about 424 cal, 37 g pro, 27 g total fat (12 g sat. fat), 6 g carb (trace dietary fibre, 7 g sugar), 175 mg chol, 409 mg sodium, 412 mg potassium. % RDI: 22% calcium, 14% iron, 19% vit A, 18% vit C, 8% folate.

Roasted Lemon and Herb Cornish Hens

p.106

HANDS-ON TIME	•	TOTAL TIME	•	MAKES
25 MINUTES		1¼ HOURS		8 SERVINGS

What you need

1 tsp	grated lemon zest
¼ cup	lemon juice
2 tbsp	olive oil
4	cloves garlic, finely grated or pressed
1 tbsp	each chopped fresh thyme and fresh oregano
2 tsp	liquid honey
1 tsp	salt
½ tsp	pepper
4	Cornish hens (each about 580 g)
1	lemon, halved crosswise

How to make it

In large bowl, whisk together lemon zest, lemon juice, oil, garlic, thyme, oregano, honey, salt and pepper. Set aside. *(Make-ahead: Cover and refrigerate for up to 24 hours; whisk again before using.)*

Using kitchen shears, cut 1 hen down each side of backbone; discard backbone or reserve for another use. Cut hen in half lengthwise through breastbone. Repeat with remaining hens. *(Make-ahead: Cover and refrigerate for up to 24 hours.)*

Add hens to lemon mixture; toss to coat. Arrange, skin side up, on lightly greased large heavy-duty rimmed baking sheet. Add lemon, cut side up.

Roast in 425°F (220°C) oven, basting twice, until instant-read thermometer inserted in thickest part of thigh reads 185°F (85°C), about 45 minutes. Remove hens to platter. Let stand for 5 minutes.

Meanwhile, return lemon to oven; broil, cut side up, until lightly charred, about 1 minute. Serve with hens.

TIP FROM THE TEST KITCHEN

Splitting the hens in half helps them cook more evenly and crisps more of the skin. You can use also split larger chickens or even turkeys.

NUTRITIONAL INFORMATION, PER SERVING: about 333 cal, 25 g pro, 24 g total fat (6 g sat. fat), 3 g carb (trace dietary fibre, 2 g sugar), 146 mg chol, 359 mg sodium, 304 mg potassium. % RDI: 2% calcium, 9% iron, 4% vit A, 13% vit C, 2% folate.

Ribs With Blackberry Sauce

HANDS-ON TIME	•	TOTAL TIME	•	MAKES
30 MINUTES		6 HOURS		ABOUT 24 PIECES

What you need

1.35 kg	pork back ribs
2 tbsp	chili powder
1 tbsp	dry mustard
3	cloves garlic, minced
¾ tsp	each salt and cinnamon
½ cup	blackberry jam
¼ cup	ketchup
1 tbsp	balsamic vinegar
2 tsp	minced peeled fresh ginger
¼ tsp	pepper

How to make it

Remove membrane from underside of ribs, if attached. Pour enough water into shallow roasting pan to come scant ½ inch (1 cm) up sides. Add ribs, meaty side up. Cover and bake in 325°F (160°C) oven until meat is tender, 80 to 90 minutes. Using tongs, transfer ribs to cutting board. Let stand for 10 minutes. Cut into 1-rib portions.

In large bowl, combine chili powder, mustard, garlic, salt and cinnamon. Add ribs, rubbing, to coat. Cover and refrigerate for 4 hours. (*Make-ahead: Refrigerate for up to 24 hours.*)

Meanwhile, in small saucepan, combine blackberry jam, ketchup, vinegar, ginger and pepper; bring to boil. Reduce heat to simmer; cook, stirring often, for 5 minutes. Strain through fine-mesh sieve into bowl, pressing on solids. Set aside. (*Make-ahead: Let cool; refrigerate in airtight container for up to 1 week.*)

Place ribs, meaty side down, on lightly greased rack on foil-lined rimmed baking sheet. Broil for 5 minutes.

Brush ribs with half of the blackberry sauce; broil until bubbling, about 2 minutes. Turn and brush with remaining sauce; broil until sauce bubbles, about 2 minutes.

TIP FROM THE TEST KITCHEN

Ribs often have a tough membrane still attached to the underside, which should be removed before marinating or cooking. Lift up a corner of the membrane, then pull it off. If you have trouble grabbing the membrane (it can be slippery), hold it with a paper towel.

NUTRITIONAL INFORMATION, PER PIECE: about 103 cal, 6 g pro, 6 g total fat (2 g sat. fat), 6 g carb (trace dietary fibre), 14 mg chol, 118 mg sodium. % RDI: 1% calcium, 3% iron, 2% vit A, 3% vit C, 2% folate.

Roast Pork With Cider Cream Sauce

HANDS-ON TIME	•	TOTAL TIME	•	MAKES
25 MINUTES		4 HOURS		8 SERVINGS

What you need

PORK
2 tbsp	vegetable oil
3	cloves garlic, minced
1 tbsp	each finely chopped fresh sage and thyme (or ½ tsp each crumbled dried sage and dried thyme)
1 tsp	salt
½ tsp	pepper
1.35 kg	boneless pork loin centre roast, rolled and tied

CIDER CREAM SAUCE
2 tbsp	butter
2	Granny Smith apples, peeled, quartered, cored, and thinly sliced crosswise
1	onion, diced
1 cup	alcoholic or nonalcoholic apple cider
1 cup	sodium-reduced chicken broth
¾ cup	whipping cream (35%)
1 tbsp	grainy or Dijon mustard
1 tsp	cornstarch

How to make it

PORK: Stir together oil, garlic, sage, thyme, salt and pepper; rub all over roast. Cover and refrigerate for 2 hours. *(Make-ahead: Refrigerate for up to 24 hours.)*

Place roast on lightly greased rack in roasting pan. Roast in 375°F (190°C) oven until instant-read thermometer inserted into centre reads 160°F (71°C), about 90 minutes. Transfer to cutting board; cover loosely with foil and let stand for 15 minutes before slicing.

CIDER CREAM SAUCE: Meanwhile, skim fat from pan juices. Add butter and cook over medium heat until melted. Add apples and onion; cook, stirring often, for 5 minutes. Stir in cider and bring to boil, scraping up browned bits. Stir in broth, cream and mustard; cook until reduced by half, about 8 minutes.

In small bowl, mix cornstarch with 1 tbsp water; whisk into apple mixture. Cook, stirring, until thickened, about 1 minute. Serve with pork.

TIP FROM THE TEST KITCHEN

The best way to avoid dry, overcooked meat is to use an instant-read digital thermometer. Insert the probe into the thickest part of a roast to check its internal temperature. If you're cooking a bone-in roast, be sure the probe isn't touching a bone (which can skew the reading).

NUTRITIONAL INFORMATION, PER SERVING: about 397 cal, 34 g pro, 23 g total fat (10 g sat. fat), 11 g carb, (1 g dietary fibre), 128 mg chol, 493 mg sodium. % RDI: 6% calcium, 11% iron, 10% vit A, 5% vit C, 4% folate.

Pork Pie With Oka Mash

HANDS-ON TIME	•	TOTAL TIME	•	MAKES
20 MINUTES		1¼ HOURS		8 TO 10 SERVINGS

What you need

How to make it

PORK PIE

1 tbsp	olive oil
2	leeks (white and light green parts only), halved lengthwise and thinly sliced
3	cloves garlic, minced
900 g	lean ground pork
115 g	dry-cured chorizo, chopped
2 cups	sodium-reduced beef broth
⅓ cup	all-purpose flour
1	sweet potato, peeled and finely chopped
1 tsp	smoked paprika
¼ tsp	each salt and pepper
pinch	cinnamon
1 cup	frozen peas

OKA MASH

1.35 kg	yellow-fleshed or russet potatoes, peeled and quartered
2	cloves garlic
1 cup	milk
225 g	shredded Oka cheese
2 tbsp	butter

PORK PIE: In large saucepan, heat oil over medium heat; cook leeks and garlic, stirring occasionally, until softened, about 6 minutes. Transfer to bowl.

In same pan, cook pork and chorizo over medium-high heat, breaking up pork with spoon, until pork is no longer pink, about 5 minutes. Add ¼ cup of the broth; cook, scraping up browned bits, until no liquid remains. Stir in flour; cook, stirring, for 2 minutes.

Gradually stir in remaining broth; bring to boil. Stir in leek mixture, sweet potato, paprika, salt, pepper and cinnamon; return to boil. Reduce heat to simmer; cook, stirring often, until slightly thickened, about 15 minutes. Stir in peas; scrape into 13- x 9-inch (3 L) baking dish.

OKA MASH: Meanwhile, in large saucepan of boiling salted water, cook potatoes and garlic until tender, about 20 minutes. Drain and return to pan; mash with milk, Oka and butter. Spread over pork mixture.

Bake in 400°F (200°C) oven until filling is bubbly and topping is golden, about 25 minutes.

TIP FROM THE TEST KITCHEN

You can easily freeze this dish for up to 2 months. Follow first 4 paragraphs. Let cool. Cover with plastic wrap and overwrap in heavy-duty foil; freeze. Thaw in refrigerator for 24 hours; remove plastic wrap, re-cover with foil and bake in 400°F (200°C) oven for 35 minutes. Increase heat to 425°F (220°C) and remove foil; bake until topping is golden, about 10 minutes.

NUTRITIONAL INFORMATION, PER EACH OF 10 SERVINGS: about 523 cal, 30 g pro, 29 g total fat (13 g sat. fat), 34 g carb (3 g dietary fibre), 105 mg chol, 549 mg sodium, 841 mg potassium. % RDI: 20% calcium, 17% iron, 47% vit A, 23% vit C, 19% folate.

Slow Cooker Dal

p.4

HANDS-ON TIME	•	TOTAL TIME	•	MAKES
20 MINUTES		8¼ HOURS		6 TO 8 SERVINGS

What you need

2	onions
2 cups	dried green lentils, rinsed
2	tomatoes, seeded and chopped
1	jalapeño pepper, seeded and sliced
4	cloves garlic, minced
4 tsp	minced peeled fresh ginger
1 tbsp	each cumin seeds and ground coriander
¼ cup	butter
1 tbsp	lemon juice
1½ tsp	salt
½ tsp	pepper
½ cup	plain Balkan-style yogurt
¼ cup	chopped fresh cilantro

How to make it

Slice 1 of the onions; set aside. Finely chop remaining onion.

In slow cooker, combine chopped onion, lentils, half of the tomatoes, the jalapeño pepper, garlic, ginger, half each of the cumin seeds and coriander and 6 cups water. Cover and cook on low until lentils are tender, 8 to 10 hours.

Using immersion blender, purée mixture to desired consistency and thickness, leaving some lentils whole. *(Make-ahead: Refrigerate in airtight container for up to 24 hours or freeze for up to 3 weeks; reheat before continuing with recipe.)*

Meanwhile, in skillet, melt butter over medium heat; cook sliced onion, stirring, until dark golden, about 7 minutes. Add remaining cumin seeds and coriander; cook, stirring, until fragrant, about 1 minute. Stir in lemon juice, salt and pepper.

Stir onion mixture into slow cooker. Serve with yogurt, cilantro and remaining tomatoes.

TIP FROM THE TEST KITCHEN

If you don't have an immersion blender, transfer one-third of the lentil mixture to a blender, purée until smooth and then stir the purée back into the slow cooker.

NUTRITIONAL INFORMATION, PER EACH OF 8 SERVINGS:
about 251 cal, 14 g pro, 7 g total fat (4 g sat. fat), 35 g carb (7 g dietary fibre, 5 g sugar), 18 mg chol, 486 mg sodium, 720 mg potassium. % RDI: 6% calcium, 37% iron, 10% vit A, 18% vit C, 119% folate.

Bacon and Gouda Quiche

HANDS-ON TIME	•	TOTAL TIME	•	MAKES
45 MINUTES		2½ HOURS		8 SERVINGS

What you need

PASTRY

1½ cups	all-purpose flour
½ tsp	salt
¼ cup	each cold butter and cold lard, cubed
1	egg yolk
1 tsp	vinegar or lemon juice
	ice water

FILLING

4	strips thick-cut bacon, chopped
2 tsp	vegetable oil
6	shallots, quartered
2	cloves garlic, minced
¼ tsp	each dried thyme and pepper
pinch	salt
½ cup	chopped roasted red peppers
2 tbsp	chopped fresh chives
¾ cup	shredded aged Gouda cheese
3	eggs
¾ cup	milk

How to make it

PASTRY: In bowl, whisk flour with salt. Using pastry blender or 2 knives, cut in butter and lard until mixture resembles fine crumbs with a few larger pieces.

In liquid measure, whisk egg yolk with vinegar; add enough ice water to make ⅓ cup. Drizzle over flour mixture, stirring briskly with fork to form ragged dough. Press into disc. Wrap in plastic wrap; refrigerate until chilled, about 30 minutes. (*Make-ahead: Refrigerate for up to 3 days.*)

On lightly floured work surface, roll out pastry to scant ¼-inch (5 mm) thickness; fit into 9-inch (23 cm) quiche dish or pie plate. Trim edge, leaving 1-inch (2.5 cm) overhang; fold overhang inside rim. If using pie plate, flute edge. Prick all over with fork. Refrigerate for 30 minutes.

Line pastry shell with foil; fill with pie weights or dried beans. Bake on bottom rack of 400°F (200°C) oven until rim is light golden, about 15 minutes. Remove weights and foil; let crust cool on rack.

FILLING: While crust is baking, in large skillet, cook bacon over medium-high heat, stirring, until crisp, about 5 minutes. With slotted spoon, transfer to paper towel–lined plate to drain. Drain fat from pan.

Add oil to pan and heat over medium heat; cook shallots, garlic, thyme, pepper and salt until shallots are softened, about 10 minutes. Transfer to bowl and let cool. Stir in bacon, red peppers and chives.

Sprinkle ½ cup of the Gouda over crust. Spread bacon mixture over top. Whisk eggs with milk; pour into crust. Sprinkle with remaining Gouda.

Bake in 375°F (190°C) oven until tip of knife inserted in centre comes out clean, about 35 minutes. Let cool on rack for 10 minutes. (*Make-ahead: Wrap in plastic wrap and refrigerate for up to 24 hours, or overwrap in foil and freeze for up to 2 weeks. Thaw, if frozen. Reheat in 350°F/180°C oven for 20 minutes.*)

NUTRITIONAL INFORMATION, PER SERVING: about 287 cal, 10 g pro, 20 g total fat (9 g sat. fat), 17 g carb (1 g dietary fibre), 126 mg chol, 391 mg sodium. % RDI: 11% calcium, 10% iron, 16% vit A, 33% vit C, 25% folate.

Ham Hock Hash With Poached Eggs and Swiss Chard

HANDS-ON TIME	•	TOTAL TIME	•	MAKES
45 MINUTES		3¼ HOURS		8 SERVINGS

What you need

How to make it

HAM HOCK

900 g	smoked ham hock
1	onion, quartered
1	carrot, quartered
3	sprigs each fresh parsley and thyme
4	whole cloves
2	bay leaves
2	cloves garlic
½ tsp	black peppercorns

HASH

900 g	russet or yellow-fleshed potatoes (6 to 8), peeled and cut in ½-inch (1 cm) cubes
2 tbsp	vegetable oil
2	onions, chopped
1	pkg (227 g) cremini mushrooms, sliced
3	cloves garlic, minced
1 tsp	finely chopped fresh thyme (or ½ tsp dried thyme)
¼ tsp	each salt and pepper
¾ tsp	smoked or sweet paprika
2 tbsp	white wine vinegar
¼ cup	chopped fresh parsley

SAUTÉED SWISS CHARD

1 kg	Swiss chard, trimmed and coarsely chopped
3 tbsp	olive oil
3	cloves garlic, minced
¼ tsp	each salt and hot pepper flakes
8	eggs, poached

HAM HOCK: In large saucepan, add ham hock, onion, carrot, parsley, thyme, cloves, bay leaves, garlic, peppercorns and enough cold water to cover; bring to boil. Reduce heat to low; cover and cook for 2 hours, skimming off foam as necessary.

Transfer ham hock to bowl; let cool enough to handle. Remove skin and slice into strips; discard fat and bone. Using 2 forks, shred ham. Set aside.

Strain ham cooking liquid through fine-mesh sieve into large saucepan; skim off fat. Remove ¼ cup of the liquid to small bowl; bring remaining liquid to boil.

HASH: Add potatoes to ham cooking liquid; cook over medium-high heat just until tender, 5 to 7 minutes. Drain. (*Make-ahead: Refrigerate ham and potatoes in separate airtight containers for up to 24 hours.*)

In large heavy skillet, heat oil over medium heat; cook onions, stirring occasionally, until softened, about 5 minutes. Add mushrooms, garlic, thyme, salt and pepper; cook, stirring, until mushrooms are browned, about 8 minutes. Stir in paprika. Add vinegar and reserved ham cooking liquid, scraping up browned bits. Reduce heat to simmer; cook until no liquid remains. Add potatoes, ham skin, ham hock and parsley; cook, stirring, until heated through, about 6 minutes.

SAUTÉED SWISS CHARD: In large saucepan of boiling salted water, cook Swiss chard until tender, 2 to 4 minutes. Drain and squeeze out liquid. (*Make-ahead: Refrigerate in airtight container for up to 24 hours.*)

In large skillet, heat oil over medium-high heat. Add garlic, salt and hot pepper flakes; cook, stirring, until garlic is golden, about 20 seconds. Add Swiss chard; cook, tossing, until heated through, 3 to 5 minutes. Serve with hash and poached eggs.

NUTRITIONAL INFORMATION, PER SERVING: about 417 cal, 30 g pro, 19 g total fat (5 g sat. fat), 31 g carb (5 g dietary fibre), 231 mg chol, 284 mg sodium. % RDI: 19% calcium, 17% iron, 46% vit A, 27% vit C, 24% folate.

Apple Cheddar Quick Bread

HANDS-ON TIME
20 MINUTES

•

TOTAL TIME
1½ HOURS

•

MAKES
12 TO 16 SLICES

What you need

2 cups	all-purpose flour
1 tsp	baking powder
½ tsp	baking soda
¼ tsp	salt
1⅓ cups	shredded extra-old Cheddar cheese
⅓ cup	butter, softened
⅔ cup	granulated sugar
2	eggs
1 cup	diced cored peeled Granny Smith apple
¾ cup	grated peeled Granny Smith apple
⅔ cup	milk

How to make it

In large bowl, whisk together flour, baking powder, baking soda and salt; stir in 1 cup of the Cheddar.

In separate bowl, beat butter until smooth; beat in sugar. Beat in eggs, 1 at a time. Stir in diced apple, grated apple and milk; stir into flour mixture just until combined. Scrape into greased 9- x 5-inch (2 L) loaf pan, smoothing top; sprinkle with remaining Cheddar.

Bake in 375°F (190°C) oven until Cheddar on top is melted and golden, and cake tester inserted in centre comes out clean, 50 to 55 minutes. Let cool in pan on rack for 10 minutes. Turn out onto rack; let cool completely. *(Make-ahead: Wrap in plastic wrap and store for up to 2 days, or overwrap in foil and freeze for up to 1 month.)*

TIP FROM THE TEST KITCHEN

Baking powder and baking soda can lose effectiveness over time. To test baking powder, spoon a little into a heatproof bowl and pour in some boiling water. If it bubbles vigorously, it's still active. Use the same test for baking soda, replacing the boiling water with vinegar.

NUTRITIONAL INFORMATION, PER EACH OF 16 SLICES:
about 182 cal, 5 g pro, 8 g total fat (5 g sat. fat), 22 g carb (1 g dietary fibre, 11 g sugar), 44 mg chol, 193 mg sodium, 61 mg potassium. % RDI: 9% calcium, 6% iron, 8% vit A, 13% folate.

Cinnamon Streusel Loaf

HANDS-ON TIME	TOTAL TIME	MAKES
20 MINUTES	1½ HOURS	12 SLICES

What you need

STREUSEL

¾ cup	packed light brown sugar
⅔ cup	all-purpose flour
½ tsp	cinnamon
½ cup	cold butter, cubed

LOAF

½ cup	butter, softened
¾ cup	granulated sugar
2	eggs
2 tsp	vanilla
2¼ cups	all-purpose flour
1 tsp	baking powder
½ tsp	each baking soda and salt
⅔ cup	buttermilk

How to make it

STREUSEL: In small bowl, stir together brown sugar, flour and cinnamon. Using pastry blender or 2 knives, cut in butter until crumbly; set aside.

LOAF: In large bowl, beat butter with sugar until light and fluffy; beat in eggs, 1 at a time. Beat in vanilla. In separate bowl, whisk together flour, baking powder, baking soda and salt; stir into butter mixture, alternating with buttermilk, making 3 additions of flour mixture and 2 of buttermilk.

Scrape half of the batter into parchment paper–lined 9- x 5-inch (2 L) loaf pan. Top with half of the streusel. Scrape remaining batter over top, smoothing top; sprinkle with remaining streusel.

Bake in 325°F (160°C) oven until cake tester inserted in centre comes out clean, about 65 minutes. Let cool in pan on rack for 10 minutes. Turn out onto rack; let cool completely. (*Make-ahead: Wrap in plastic wrap and store for up to 2 days, or overwrap in foil and freeze for up to 1 month.*)

TIP FROM THE TEST KITCHEN

Once you've mixed a cake or quick bread batter that's leavened with baking powder or baking soda, bake it right away. The leavening agents start to activate as soon as they're mixed with liquid; if you wait too long, your baked goods won't rise properly in the oven.

NUTRITIONAL INFORMATION, PER SLICE: about 367 cal, 5 g pro, 17 g total fat (10 g sat. fat), 50 g carb (1 g dietary fibre, 27 g sugar), 73 mg chol, 310 mg sodium, 121 mg potassium. % RDI: 5% calcium, 13% iron, 15% vit A, 30% folate.

Gluten-Free Cherry Almond Muffins

HANDS-ON TIME	•	TOTAL TIME	•	MAKES
10 MINUTES		35 MINUTES		12 MUFFINS

What you need

½ cup	unsweetened medium shredded coconut
½ cup	brown rice flour
¼ cup	each almond flour, cornstarch and tapioca starch
2 tsp	baking powder
¾ tsp	baking soda
½ tsp	xanthan gum
¼ tsp	salt
¾ cup	dried cherries, chopped
⅓ cup	natural (skin-on) almonds, chopped
¾ cup	2% plain Greek yogurt
½ cup	granulated sugar
¼ cup	light-tasting olive oil or safflower oil
2	eggs
1 tsp	each cider vinegar and vanilla

How to make it

In small skillet, toast coconut over medium heat, stirring often, until light golden, about 5 minutes. Set aside.

In large bowl, whisk together brown rice flour, almond flour, cornstarch, tapioca starch, baking powder, baking soda, xanthan gum and salt; stir in coconut, cherries and almonds.

In separate large bowl, whisk together yogurt, sugar, oil, eggs, vinegar and vanilla. Add flour mixture; stir just until combined. Spoon into 12 paper-lined wells of muffin pan.

Bake in 350°F (180°C) oven until tops are firm to the touch, about 20 minutes. Let cool in pan on rack for 5 minutes; transfer to rack and let cool. *(Make-ahead: Store in airtight container for up to 3 days. Or wrap individually in plastic wrap and freeze in airtight container for up to 1 month.)*

TIP FROM THE TEST KITCHEN

Almond flour is very finely ground (powdery) skinned almonds. Look for it in bags in the natural food section of your grocery store. Almond meal is coarser— not the right texture for these muffins.

NUTRITIONAL INFORMATION, PER MUFFIN: about 227 cal, 5 g pro, 11 g total fat (4 g sat. fat), 29 g carb (2 g dietary fibre, 16 g sugar), 32 mg chol, 206 mg sodium, 122 mg potassium. % RDI: 7% calcium, 6% iron, 3% vit A, 3% folate.

Mini Corn Muffins

HANDS-ON TIME	•	**TOTAL TIME**	•	**MAKES**
15 MINUTES		25 MINUTES		24 MUFFINS

What you need

1 cup	medium-ground cornmeal
¼ cup	all-purpose flour
2 tbsp	granulated sugar
½ tsp	baking soda
¼ tsp	salt
pinch	cayenne pepper
1 cup	buttermilk
1	egg
2 tbsp	butter, melted
⅔ cup	frozen corn kernels, thawed

How to make it

In large bowl, whisk together cornmeal, flour, sugar, baking soda, salt and cayenne pepper.

In separate bowl, whisk together buttermilk, egg and butter; pour over cornmeal mixture. Add corn; stir just until combined. Spoon into 24 greased wells of mini muffin pans.

Bake in 400°F (200°C) oven until toothpick inserted in a few comes out clean, about 10 minutes. Let cool in pan on rack. *(Make-ahead: Store in airtight container for up to 2 days or freeze for up to 2 weeks.)*

TIP FROM THE TEST KITCHEN

Medium-ground cornmeal gives these muffins a slightly crunchy texture. Look for it in the health foods section of grocery stores or in bulk food stores.

NUTRITIONAL INFORMATION, PER MUFFIN: about 48 cal, 1 g pro, 2 g total fat (1 g sat. fat), 7 g carb (1 g dietary fibre, 2 g sugar), 11 mg chol, 69 mg sodium, 49 mg potassium. % RDI: 2% calcium, 1% iron, 2% vit A, 3% folate.

Mini Lemon Scones
With Strawberries and Cream

HANDS-ON TIME
25 MINUTES

•

TOTAL TIME
40 MINUTES

•

MAKES
ABOUT 24 PIECES

What you need

STRAWBERRIES
2 cups	sliced hulled strawberries
1 tbsp	granulated sugar
1 tsp	grated lemon zest

SCONES
2½ cups	all-purpose flour
2 tbsp	granulated sugar
1 tbsp	grated lemon zest
2½ tsp	baking powder
½ tsp	each baking soda and salt
½ cup	cold butter, cubed
1 cup	buttermilk
1	egg

TOPPING
1	egg, lightly beaten
2 tsp	granulated sugar
1	bottle (170 g) Devonshire cream (or 1 cup whipped cream)

How to make it

STRAWBERRIES: In bowl, combine strawberries, sugar and lemon zest; cover and refrigerate until chilled. *(Make-ahead: Refrigerate for up to 6 hours.)*

SCONES: Meanwhile, in large bowl, whisk together flour, sugar, lemon zest, baking powder, baking soda and salt. Using pastry blender or 2 knives, cut in butter until mixture resembles coarse crumbs. Whisk buttermilk with egg; add to flour mixture, stirring with fork to make soft dough.

With lightly floured hands, press dough into ball. On floured work surface, knead gently 10 times. Pat out into scant ¾-inch (2 cm) thick round. Using 1¾-inch (4.5 cm) floured round or fluted cookie cutter, cut out rounds, patting out scraps as necessary. Place on parchment paper–lined rimless baking sheets.

TOPPING: Brush tops of biscuits with egg; sprinkle with sugar. Bake, 1 sheet at a time, in 400°F (200°C) oven until golden, about 12 minutes. Let cool on pans on racks. *(Make-ahead: Store in airtight container for up to 24 hours or wrap in plastic wrap and freeze in airtight container for up to 2 weeks.)* Serve with strawberry mixture and cream.

TIP FROM THE TEST KITCHEN

Devonshire, or clotted, cream is an English specialty; cream is gently heated until it forms thick clumps (clots). It's very rich and does not need to be whipped. Look for small jars in the dairy section of the grocery store.

NUTRITIONAL INFORMATION, PER PIECE: about 135 cal, 3 g pro, 8 g total fat (5 g sat. fat), 14 g carb (1g dietary fibre), 37 mg chol, 162 mg sodium. % RDI: 3% calcium, 5% iron, 7% vit A, 15% vit C, 15% folate.

The Ultimate Pizza Dough

HANDS-ON TIME 15 MINUTES	•	**TOTAL TIME** 24¼ HOURS	•	**MAKES** 1 CRUST

What you need

2 cups	all-purpose flour (approx)
1 tsp	quick-rising (instant) dry yeast
½ tsp	salt
⅔ cup	warm water
2 tsp	olive oil

How to make it

In large bowl, whisk together 1½ cups of the flour, the yeast and salt. Using wooden spoon, stir in warm water and olive oil until ragged dough forms.

Turn out onto lightly floured surface; knead, adding as much of the remaining flour, a little at a time, as necessary to prevent sticking, until smooth and elastic, about 8 minutes. (Dough will be slightly tacky, but won't stick to hands or work surface.)

Transfer to greased bowl; turn dough to grease all over. Cover with plastic wrap. Refrigerate for 24 hours. (Or let rise in warm, draft-free place until doubled in bulk, about 1½ hours.)

TO MAKE 12-INCH (30 CM) REGULAR PIZZA: On lightly floured surface, roll out dough into 12-inch (30 cm) circle; transfer to greased pizza pan. Add desired toppings. Bake on bottom rack in 500°F (260°C) oven until crust is golden, about 15 minutes.

TO MAKE 14-INCH (35 CM) THIN-CRUST PIZZA: On lightly floured surface, roll out dough into 14-inch (35 cm) circle; transfer to greased pizza pan. Add desired toppings. Bake on bottom rack in 500°F (260°C) oven until crust is golden, 12 to 15 minutes.

TIP FROM THE TEST KITCHEN
Letting the dough rise very slowly in the refrigerator for 24 hours greatly improves both its texture and flavour.

NUTRITIONAL INFORMATION, PER EACH OF 8 SLICES OF CRUST (WITHOUT TOPPINGS): about 125 cal, 4 g pro, 2 g total fat (trace sat. fat), 23 g carb (1 g dietary fibre, trace sugar), 0 mg chol, 144 mg sodium, 40 mg potassium. % RDI: 1% calcium, 11% iron, 23% folate.

Easy No-Knead
White Sandwich Bread

HANDS-ON TIME	TOTAL TIME	MAKES
15 MINUTES	14¾ HOURS	2 LOAVES, EACH 16 SLICES

What you need

6 cups	white bread flour (approx)
2 tsp	salt
1 tsp	quick-rising (instant) dry yeast
2½ cups	lukewarm water

How to make it

In large bowl, whisk together 5 cups of the flour, the salt and yeast. Stir in lukewarm water until well combined. Cover with plastic wrap; let rise in warm draft-free place until bubbly and doubled in bulk, about 12 hours. (*Make-ahead: Let rise for up to 18 hours.*)

Sprinkle work surface with ⅓ cup of the remaining flour. Scrape dough onto work surface; sprinkle ¼ cup of the remaining flour over top. Cover with tea towel; let stand for 15 minutes.

Using floured hands, gently press dough out into ½-inch (1 cm) thick rectangle, sprinkling with up to ¼ cup of the remaining flour if dough is too sticky.

Cut in half crosswise. Roll each half into scant 8- x 4-inch (20 x 10 cm) cylinder; place, seam side down, in greased nonstick 8- x 4-inch (1.5 L) loaf pan. Cover loosely with lightly greased plastic wrap; let rise in warm draft-free place until almost doubled in bulk, about 1½ hours.

Bake in 425°F (220°C) oven for 10 minutes. Decrease heat to 375°F (190°C); bake until light golden and loaves sound hollow when tapped, about 30 minutes.

Transfer to racks; serve warm or let cool. (*Make-ahead: Let cool completely. Slice loaves; wrap in plastic wrap and freeze in resealable freezer bag for up to 3 weeks.*)

TIP FROM THE TEST KITCHEN

Let the loaf cool completely before slicing and freezing; this helps ensure the slices will be moist when you thaw them.

NUTRITIONAL INFORMATION, PER SLICE: about 93 cal, 4 g pro, 1 g total fat (trace sat. fat), 18 g carb (1 g dietary fibre, trace sugar), 0 mg chol, 144 mg sodium, 35 mg potassium. % RDI: 9% iron, 18% folate.

Easy No-Knead
Whole Wheat Sandwich Bread

HANDS-ON TIME	•	TOTAL TIME	•	MAKES
15 MINUTES		14¾ HOURS		2 LOAVES, EACH 16 SLICES

What you need

2 tbsp	sesame seeds
1 tbsp	poppy seeds
¼ tsp	whole flaxseeds (optional)
3 cups	whole wheat bread flour
3 cups	white bread flour (approx)
2 tsp	salt
1 tsp	quick-rising (instant) dry yeast
2½ cups	lukewarm water

How to make it

Stir ¼ tsp of the sesame seeds with ¼ tsp of the poppy seeds; stir in flaxseeds (if using). Set aside. In large bowl, whisk together whole wheat flour, 2 cups of the white flour, remaining sesame seeds and poppy seeds, salt and yeast. Stir in lukewarm water until well combined. Cover with plastic wrap; let rise in warm draft-free place until bubbly and doubled in bulk, about 12 hours. (*Make-ahead: Let rise for up to 18 hours.*)

Sprinkle work surface with ⅓ cup of the remaining flour. Scrape dough onto work surface; sprinkle ¼ cup of the remaining flour over top. Cover with tea towel; let stand for 15 minutes.

Using floured hands, gently press out dough into ½-inch (1 cm) thick rectangle, sprinkling with up to ¼ cup of the remaining flour if dough is too sticky.

Cut in half crosswise. Roll each half into scant 8- x 4-inch (20 x 10 cm) cylinder; place, seam side down, in greased nonstick 8- x 4-inch (1.5 L) loaf pan. Sprinkle loaves with reserved sesame seed mixture. Cover loosely with lightly greased plastic wrap; let rise in warm draft-free place until almost doubled in bulk, about 1½ hours.

Bake in 425°F (220°C) oven for 10 minutes. Decrease heat to 375°F (190°C); bake until light golden and loaves sound hollow when tapped, about 30 minutes.

Transfer to racks; serve warm or let cool. (*Make-ahead: Let cool completely. Slice loaves; wrap in plastic wrap and freeze in resealable freezer bag for up to 3 weeks.*)

NUTRITIONAL INFORMATION, PER SLICE: about 95 cal, 4 g pro, 1 g total fat (trace sat. fat), 18 g carb (2 g dietary fibre, trace sugar), 0 mg chol, 146 mg sodium, 23 mg potassium. % RDI: 1% calcium, 8% iron, 10% folate.

The Ultimate Pull-Apart Dinner Rolls

HANDS-ON TIME
20 MINUTES

•

TOTAL TIME
4½ HOURS

•

MAKES
20 ROLLS

What you need

3 tbsp	granulated sugar
1½ cups	milk
⅓ cup	butter
1½ tsp	salt
1 tbsp	active dry yeast
1	egg
4½ cups	all-purpose flour (approx)

How to make it

Set aside 1½ tsp of the sugar. In saucepan, heat together 1¼ cups of the milk, ¼ cup of the butter, the remaining sugar and the salt over medium heat until butter is melted. Let cool to lukewarm, about 25 minutes.

Meanwhile, in small saucepan, heat remaining milk over medium heat until warm; pour into large bowl. Stir in reserved sugar until dissolved; sprinkle yeast over top. Let stand until frothy, about 10 minutes. Whisk in butter mixture and egg. Stir in 4 cups of the flour, 1 cup at a time, until soft ragged dough forms.

Turn out onto lightly floured work surface; knead, adding as much of the remaining flour as necessary to prevent sticking, until smooth and elastic, about 10 minutes. Transfer to large greased bowl; turn dough to grease all over. Cover with plastic wrap or tea towel; let rise in warm draft-free place until doubled in bulk, about 1½ hours.

Punch down dough. Turn out onto lightly floured work surface; divide dough evenly into 20 pieces. Shape 1 piece into ball, folding ends underneath and pinching at bottom; roll on work surface in circular motion, seam side down, into smooth ball. Repeat with remaining dough pieces.

Place 2 balls of dough in centre of each of 2 greased 9-inch (1.5 L) round cake pans. Place 8 balls around centre of each. Cover with tea towel; let rise in warm draft-free place until doubled in bulk, about 1 hour. Dust with flour.

Bake in 375°F (190°C) oven until rolls are golden and sound hollow when tapped, about 20 minutes. Let cool in pans for 10 minutes; transfer directly to racks. Melt remaining butter; brush over tops of rolls. *(Make-ahead: Store in airtight container for up to 24 hours. Or freeze in resealable freezer bag for up to 1 week; thaw in bag at room temperature. Reheat in 325°F/160°C oven until warm, about 5 minutes.)*

NUTRITIONAL INFORMATION, PER ROLL: about 148 cal, 5 g pro, 4 g total fat (2 g sat. fat), 23 g carb (1 g dietary fibre, 3 g sugar), 19 mg chol, 205 mg sodium, 69 mg potassium. % RDI: 3% calcium, 11% iron, 4% vit A, 26% folate.

SERVING SUGGESTION
If you prefer a dairy-free version of
these fluffy rolls, replace the milk
with almond milk and the butter
with olive oil. Add an extra pinch of
salt to the milk mixture.

Tomatillo Salsa

HANDS-ON TIME 40 MINUTES	**TOTAL TIME** 2 HOURS	**MAKES** 8 CUPS

What you need

4	sweet green peppers (900 g)
6	jalapeño peppers
6 cups	chopped tomatillos (about 900 g)
2 cups	chopped white onions
4	cloves garlic, minced
⅔ cup	white wine vinegar
3½ tsp	salt
1 tbsp	granulated sugar
1 tsp	each ground coriander and ground cumin
¼ tsp	pepper
¾ cup	finely chopped fresh cilantro
½ cup	finely chopped fresh parsley
¼ cup	lime juice

How to make it

On baking sheet, roast green peppers and jalapeño peppers in 475°F (240°C) oven, turning once, until charred, about 30 minutes. Let cool. Peel, seed and chop.

In large saucepan, combine green peppers and jalapeño peppers, tomatillos, onions, garlic, vinegar, salt, sugar, coriander, cumin and pepper; bring to boil, stirring Reduce heat to medium; cover and simmer for 5 minutes. Uncover and simmer, stirring occasionally, until no longer watery, about 30 minutes.

Stir in cilantro, parsley and lime juice; simmer for 3 minutes.

Ladle salsa into 8 hot (sterilized) 1-cup (250 ml) canning jars, leaving ½-inch (1 cm) headspace. Cover with lids; screw on bands until resistance is met. Increase to fingertip tight. Process jars in boiling water bath for 20 minutes.

Turn off heat. Uncover canner and let jars stand in canner for 5 minutes. Lift up rack. With canning tongs, transfer jars to rack to let cool, about 24 hours.

TIP FROM THE TEST KITCHEN
Check that the lids on the jars curve downward, which indicates a good seal. If any do not, refrigerate those jars and use the salsa within three weeks.

NUTRITIONAL INFORMATION, PER 1 TBSP: about 5 cal, trace pro, trace total fat (0 g sat. fat), 1 g carb (trace dietary fibre), 0 mg chol, 63 mg sodium, 31 mg potassium. % RDI: 1% iron, 1% vit A, 7% vit C, 1% folate.

Zesty Tomato Jam

HANDS-ON TIME	•	TOTAL TIME	•	MAKES
40 MINUTES		2¾ HOURS		2 CUPS

What you need

1.125 kg	ripe tomatoes (about 8 medium)
1 tbsp	olive oil
1	onion, finely diced
3	cloves garlic, minced
1½ tsp	pickling spice
¼ cup	balsamic vinegar
3 tbsp	packed brown sugar
½ tsp	each salt and pepper

How to make it

Score an X in bottom of each tomato; plunge into large saucepan of boiling water until skins start to loosen, about 12 seconds. Using slotted spoon, transfer to bowl of ice water and chill for 20 seconds; drain. Peel off skins; core and chop to make 4½ cups. Set aside.

In large shallow saucepan, heat oil over medium heat; cook onion, garlic and pickling spice, stirring often, until onion is tender, about 3 minutes.

Add tomatoes, vinegar, sugar, salt and pepper; cook, stirring occasionally, until thickened and reduced to about 2 cups, about 30 minutes. Let cool. *(Make-ahead: Refrigerate in airtight containers for up to 3 weeks or freeze for up to 3 months.)*

TIP FROM THE TEST KITCHEN
Use this sweet, tangy and chunky sauce as you would ketchup. It makes a flavourful dip, sandwich spread or accompaniment to grilled meat or fried eggs.

NUTRITIONAL INFORMATION, PER 1 TBSP: about 17 cal, trace pro, 1 g total fat (trace sat. fat), 3 g carb (trace dietary fibre, 2 g sugar), 0 mg chol, 38 mg sodium, 70 mg potassium. % RDI: 1% calcium, 1% iron, 2% vit A, 5% vit C, 1% folate.

Honey Ketchup

HANDS-ON TIME 25 MINUTES	•	**TOTAL TIME** 50 MINUTES	•	**MAKES** ABOUT 1 CUP

What you need

1 tbsp	olive oil
1	small onion, diced
1	rib celery, diced
565 g	plum tomatoes, coarsely chopped (about 5)
3 tbsp	red wine vinegar
2 tbsp	liquid honey
1 tsp	each dry mustard and garlic powder
¼ tsp	each salt and pepper
pinch	ground cloves

How to make it

In saucepan, heat oil over medium heat; cook onion and celery, stirring occasionally, until softened and light golden, about 6 minutes.

Stir in tomatoes, vinegar, honey, dry mustard, garlic powder, salt, pepper and cloves; bring to boil. Reduce heat to simmer; cover and cook for 10 minutes. Uncover and simmer until thickened and almost no liquid remains, 25 to 30 minutes.

In blender or using immersion blender, purée until smooth; press through fine sieve. Serve warm or at room temperature. *(Make-ahead: Refrigerate in airtight container for up to 1 week.)*

NUTRITIONAL INFORMATION, PER 1 TBSP: about 22 cal, trace pro, 1 g total fat (trace sat. fat), 3 g carb (trace dietary fibre, 3 g sugar), 0 mg chol, 39 mg sodium, 61 mg potassium. % RDI: 1% iron, 2% vit A, 5% vit C, 1% folate.

Quick Zucchini Relish

HANDS-ON TIME
25 MINUTES

•

TOTAL TIME
2 HOURS

•

MAKES
2 CUPS

What you need

2 tsp	vegetable oil
1	small onion, finely diced
½ tsp	yellow mustard seeds
½ tsp	ground ginger
¼ tsp	turmeric
¼ tsp	each salt and pepper
pinch	hot pepper flakes
2	zucchini (about 340 g total), finely diced
half	sweet red pepper, finely diced
3 tbsp	cider vinegar
1 tbsp	packed brown sugar
2 tsp	cornstarch

How to make it

In saucepan, heat oil over medium heat; cook onion, mustard seeds, ginger, turmeric, salt, pepper and hot pepper flakes, stirring often, until onion is softened, about 6 minutes.

Stir in zucchini, red pepper, vinegar and brown sugar; cook, stirring, for 2 minutes. Stir in ½ cup water; bring to boil. Reduce heat to simmer; cover and cook, stirring occasionally, until zucchini is tender, about 10 minutes.

Whisk cornstarch with 1 tbsp water; stir into zucchini mixture. Cook, stirring, until thickened, about 2 minutes.

Pour into airtight container. Let cool completely. *(Make-ahead: Cover and refrigerate for up to 2 weeks.)*

TIP FROM THE TEST KITCHEN
This small-batch relish doesn't need to be processed in a boiling water canner—just refrigerate it in an airtight container.

NUTRITIONAL INFORMATION, PER 1 TBSP: about 8 cal, trace pro, trace total fat (0 g sat. fat), 1 g carb (trace dietary fibre, 1 g sugar), 0 mg chol, 19 mg sodium, 32 mg potassium. % RDI: 1% iron, 2% vit A, 7% vit C, 1% folate.

SERVING SUGGESTION

Serve this **Quick Zucchini Relish** with **The Ultimate Pub-Style Burger** (recipe, page 46), grilled chicken or pork, sausages, or even in place of salsa with tortilla chips.

Spiced Peach Chutney

HANDS-ON TIME	•	TOTAL TIME	•	MAKES
25 MINUTES		2 HOURS		3 CUPS

What you need | How to make it

4	firm ripe peaches
2 tsp	vegetable oil
1	onion, chopped
1 tbsp	minced seeded jalapeño pepper
2 tsp	minced fresh ginger
¼ tsp	ground coriander
pinch	cinnamon
6 tbsp	granulated sugar
3 tbsp	cider vinegar
½ tsp	each salt and pepper
1 tsp	cornstarch

Score an X in bottom of each peach; plunge into large saucepan of boiling water until skin starts to loosen, about 30 seconds. Using slotted spoon, transfer to bowl of ice water. Chill for 20 seconds; drain. Peel off skins; halve peaches and remove pits. Chop peaches into ½-inch (1 cm) chunks to make about 3 cups. Set aside.

In saucepan, heat oil over medium heat; cook onion, jalapeño pepper, ginger, coriander and cinnamon, stirring frequently, until onion is golden, about 10 minutes.

Stir in peaches, sugar, vinegar, salt, pepper and 2 tbsp water; cook, stirring, until peaches are tender but still hold their shape, about 5 minutes.

Stir cornstarch with 1 tbsp water; stir into peach mixture and cook, stirring, until thickened, about 1 minute. Let cool. (*Make-ahead: Refrigerate in airtight containers for up to 3 weeks or freeze for up to 2 months.*)

NUTRITIONAL INFORMATION, PER 1 TBSP: about 13 cal, trace pro, trace total fat (0 g sat. fat), 3 g carb (trace dietary fibre, 3 g sugar), 0 mg chol, 24 mg sodium, 25 mg potassium. % RDI: 2% vit C.

Easy Blueberry Lemon Spread

HANDS-ON TIME	•	TOTAL TIME	•	MAKES
20 MINUTES		2 HOURS		1½ CUPS

What you need

1	lemon
2 cups	wild blueberries
2 cups	granulated sugar
pinch	salt

How to make it

Finely grate lemon zest and juice lemon. Place seeds on square of cheesecloth; gather corners and tie together with butcher's twine. Set aside.

In saucepan, lightly crush blueberries with potato masher. Add sugar, 2 tbsp of the lemon juice, 2 tsp of the lemon zest and the salt. Cook over medium heat, stirring constantly, until sugar is dissolved.

Add cheesecloth pouch. Boil hard for 4 minutes, skimming off foam and stirring frequently (mixture will be thin). Let cool. *(Make-ahead: Refrigerate in airtight container for up to 3 weeks or freeze for up to 2 months.)*

TIP FROM THE TEST KITCHEN
Lemon seeds are a natural source of pectin, so you don't need added pectin in this jam-like spread.

NUTRITIONAL INFORMATION, PER 1 TBSP: about 72 cal, trace pro, 0 g total fat (0 g sat. fat), 19 g carb (trace dietary fibre, 18 g sugar), 0 mg chol, 0 mg sodium, 12 mg potassium. % RDI: 2% vit C.

Hot Honey Mustard

HANDS-ON TIME	•	TOTAL TIME	•	MAKES
10 MINUTES		30 MINUTES		2 CUPS

What you need

1 cup	dry mustard
½ cup	granulated sugar
½ cup	liquid honey
¼ cup	cider vinegar
3 tbsp	canola oil
½ tsp	kosher salt
½ tsp	lemon juice

How to make it

In food processor, whirl mustard with ¼ cup cold water, scraping down side and bottom of bowl once, until thick smooth paste forms.

Add sugar, honey, vinegar, oil, salt and lemon juice. Whirl, scraping down side and bottom of bowl once, until smooth, about 1 minute.

Scrape into 4 hot (sterilized) ½-cup (125 ml) canning jars; seal. Let jars cool. Store in refrigerator. *(Make-ahead: Refrigerate for up to 6 months.)*

TIP FROM THE TEST KITCHEN

This mustard mellows as it ages; if you prefer a milder taste, let the jars stand in the fridge for a couple of weeks.

NUTRITIONAL INFORMATION, PER 1 TSP: about 18 cal, trace pro, 1 g total fat (0 g sat. fat), 3 g carb (0 g dietary fibre), 0 mg chol, 8 mg sodium, 7 mg potassium. % RDI: 1% iron.

Chocolate Hazelnut Spread

HANDS-ON TIME	•	TOTAL TIME	•	MAKES
10 MINUTES		10 MINUTES		1½ CUPS

What you need

2 cups	skinned roasted hazelnuts
½ cup	icing sugar
pinch	salt
115 g	semisweet chocolate (4 oz), melted

How to make it

In food processor, grind hazelnuts, scraping down side occasionally, into smooth paste, about 5 minutes. Add icing sugar and salt; blend, scraping down side occasionally, until smooth. Add chocolate; blend, scraping down side occasionally, until combined. *(Make-ahead: Refrigerate in airtight container for up to 2 weeks.)*

TIP FROM THE TEST KITCHEN
If you can't find skinned roasted hazelnuts, buy raw hazelnuts and roast them in a 350°F (180°C) oven until the skins crack, 8 to 10 minutes. Transfer to a tea towel and rub off as much of the skins as possible.

NUTRITIONAL INFORMATION, PER 1 TBSP: about 104 cal, 2 g pro, 8 g total fat (1 g sat. fat), 8 g carb (2 g dietary fibre, 6 g sugar), 0 mg chol, 1 mg sodium, 92 mg potassium. % RDI: 2% calcium, 4% iron, 4% folate.

Mixed Bean and Feta Salad

HANDS-ON TIME		TOTAL TIME		MAKES
10 MINUTES	•	10 MINUTES	•	6 TO 8 SERVINGS

What you need

2	cans (each 540 mL) mixed beans, drained and rinsed
2	ribs celery, diced
½ cup	crumbled feta cheese
¼ cup	each finely diced red onion, chopped fresh parsley, and red wine vinegar
3 tbsp	olive oil
½ tsp	pepper

How to make it

In large bowl, stir together beans, celery, feta, red onion, parsley, vinegar, oil and pepper. (*Make-ahead: Refrigerate in airtight container for up to 3 days. Let stand at room temperature for 15 minutes before serving.*)

TIP FROM THE TEST KITCHEN
Give this salad a quick toss just before serving to redistribute the dressing.

NUTRITIONAL INFORMATION, PER EACH OF 8 SERVINGS:
about 171 cal, 7 g pro, 8 g total fat (2 g sat. fat), 18 g carb (5 g dietary fibre, 2 g sugar), 9 mg chol, 431 mg sodium, 436 mg potassium.
% RDI: 8% calcium, 9% iron, 3% vit A, 5% vit C, 5% folate.

Bok Choy and Fennel Slaw

p.159

HANDS-ON TIME	•	TOTAL TIME	•	MAKES
15 MINUTES		4¼ HOURS		6 TO 8 SERVINGS

What you need

3 tbsp	lemon juice
2 tbsp	seasoned rice vinegar
1	small clove garlic, minced
¼ tsp	each salt and pepper
pinch	hot pepper flakes (optional)
¼ cup	extra-virgin olive oil
4	heads Shanghai bok choy (about 350 g total), thinly sliced
1	bulb fennel, cored and thinly sliced
1	carrot, cut in matchsticks

How to make it

In large bowl, whisk together lemon juice, vinegar, garlic, salt, pepper and hot pepper flakes (if using). Slowly whisk in olive oil. Add bok choy, fennel and carrot. Toss to combine. Cover and refrigerate for 4 hours. (*Make-ahead: Refrigerate for up to 24 hours.*)

TIP FROM THE TEST KITCHEN

You can eat this salad right away, but it tastes best after it has chilled for a while. Baby bok choy is an excellent substitute for Shanghai bok choy.

NUTRITIONAL INFORMATION, PER EACH OF 8 SERVINGS:
about 86 cal, 1 g pro, 7 g total fat (1 g sat. fat), 6 g carb (2 g dietary fibre, 4 g sugar), 0 mg chol., 256 mg sodium, 269 mg potassium. % RDI: 6% calcium, 5% iron, 35% vit A, 42% vit C, 18% folate.

Tangy Matchstick Salad

HANDS-ON TIME	•	TOTAL TIME	•	MAKES
40 MINUTES		1¾ HOURS		8 TO 10 SERVINGS

What you need

SALAD
6 cups	julienned peeled celery root (1 medium)
6 cups	julienned peeled beets (about 3 large)
4 cups	julienned peeled carrots (about 3 large)
⅓ cup	packed coarsely chopped fresh dill

DRESSING
⅓ cup	lemon juice
¼ cup	olive oil
1 tbsp	liquid honey
½ tsp	salt
½ cup	minced cornichons
2 tbsp	minced capers
1	shallot, minced

How to make it

SALAD: In large saucepan of boiling salted water, blanch celery root for 1 minute. With slotted spoon, remove to bowl of ice water to cool; drain. Repeat with beets, blanching for 3 minutes.

In large bowl, mix together celery root, beets, carrots and dill.

DRESSING: In small bowl, whisk together lemon juice, oil, honey and salt; stir in cornichons, capers and shallot. Pour over vegetables; toss to coat. Cover and refrigerate for 1 hour. (*Make-ahead: Refrigerate for up to 2 days.*)

TIP FROM THE TEST KITCHEN
To speed up the prep, slice the celery root and beets with a mandoline first, then cut them into matchsticks.

NUTRITIONAL INFORMATION, PER EACH OF 10 SERVINGS:
about 115 cal, 2 g pro, 6 g total fat (1 g sat. fat), 16 g carb (3 g dietary fibre, 9 g sugar), 0 mg chol, 436 mg sodium, 355 mg potassium. % RDI: 3% calcium, 6% iron, 49% vit A, 13% vit C, 21% folate.

Mediterranean Kale Salad

HANDS-ON TIME	TOTAL TIME	MAKES
10 MINUTES	2¼ HOURS	8 TO 10 SERVINGS

What you need

3 tbsp	extra-virgin olive oil
2 tbsp	balsamic vinegar
1 tsp	liquid honey
2	cloves garlic, minced
½ tsp	pepper
pinch	salt
10 cups	stemmed kale, thinly sliced
2 cups	cherry tomatoes, halved
1	can (400 mL) water-packed artichoke hearts, drained, rinsed and thinly sliced
1 cup	shaved Pecorino-Romano cheese or Parmesan cheese (about 80 g)

How to make it

In large bowl, whisk together oil, vinegar, honey, garlic, pepper and salt. Add kale, tomatoes and artichoke hearts; toss to coat.

Cover and refrigerate, tossing occasionally, until kale begins to soften slightly, about 2 hours. *(Make-ahead: Refrigerate for up to 24 hours.)*

Toss salad; sprinkle with Pecorino-Romano.

TIP FROM THE TEST KITCHEN
Use a vegetable peeler to shave the cheese for this colourful salad.

NUTRITIONAL INFORMATION, PER EACH OF 10 SERVINGS:
about 125 cal, 6 g pro, 7 g total fat (2 g sat. fat), 12 g carb (3 g dietary fibre, 4 g sugar), 8 mg chol, 213 mg sodium, 476 mg potassium.
% RDI: 18% calcium, 12% iron, 64% vit A, 145% vit C, 17% folate.

Creamy Tortellini Salad

p.117

HANDS-ON TIME	TOTAL TIME	MAKES
20 MINUTES	20 MINUTES	6 TO 8 SERVINGS

What you need

How to make it

CREAMY DRESSING

¼ cup	light mayonnaise
3 tbsp	extra-virgin olive oil
3 tbsp	red wine vinegar
1 tsp	each Dijon mustard and liquid honey
¼ tsp	pepper
pinch	salt

SALAD

1	can (400 mL) water-packed artichoke hearts, drained, chopped and patted dry
⅓ cup	drained oil-packed sun-dried tomatoes, chopped
⅓ cup	pitted Kalamata olives, chopped
2	ribs celery, thinly sliced
3	green onions, thinly sliced
2 tbsp	chopped fresh parsley
700 g	fresh cheese-filled tortellini

CREAMY DRESSING: In bowl, whisk together mayonnaise, oil, vinegar, mustard, honey, pepper and salt. Set aside. *(Make-ahead: Refrigerate in airtight container for up to 3 days.)*

SALAD: In large bowl, toss together artichokes, tomatoes, olives, celery, green onions and parsley. *(Make-ahead: Refrigerate in airtight container for up to 3 days.)*

In large saucepan of boiling salted water, cook pasta until tender and floating on surface, about 5 minutes. Drain and rinse under cold water; drain well. Add to artichoke mixture. Toss with dressing to coat.

TIP FROM THE TEST KITCHEN

You can prepare the vegetables and dressing ahead of time, but don't toss them with the cooked tortellini until you're ready to serve; the pasta will absorb too much of the dressing.

NUTRITIONAL INFORMATION, PER EACH OF 8 SERVINGS: about 390 cal, 12 g pro, 16 g total fat (3 g sat. fat), 52 g carb (4 g dietary fibre, 5 g sugar), 20 mg chol, 725 mg sodium, 218 mg potassium. % RDI: 9% calcium, 24% iron, 6% vit A, 18% vit C, 9% folate.

Yellow Bean and Rapini Salad

HANDS-ON TIME	•	TOTAL TIME	•	MAKES
20 MINUTES		20 MINUTES		10 SERVINGS

What you need

HONEY LEMON DRESSING

1 tsp	grated lemon zest (optional)
3 tbsp	lemon juice
4 tsp	liquid honey
1 tbsp	Dijon mustard
1	small clove garlic, pressed or finely grated
½ tsp	chopped fresh thyme
½ tsp	salt
¼ tsp	pepper
⅓ cup	extra-virgin olive oil

SALAD

450 g	yellow beans, trimmed and cut in 1½-inch (4 cm) lengths
1	bunch rapini, trimmed and cut in 1½-inch (4 cm) pieces
¼ cup	sliced almonds, toasted

How to make it

HONEY LEMON DRESSING: In bowl, whisk together lemon zest (if using), lemon juice, honey, mustard, garlic, thyme, salt and pepper. Gradually whisk in oil until combined. *(Make-ahead: Refrigerate in airtight container for up to 2 days.)*

SALAD: In large saucepan of boiling lightly salted water, cook beans until tender-crisp, about 2 minutes. Using slotted spoon, transfer to large bowl of ice water to chill; drain and pat dry. *(Make-ahead: Refrigerate in airtight container for up to 24 hours.)*

In same saucepan of boiling water, cook rapini just until tender, about 2 minutes. Transfer to large bowl of ice water to chill; drain and pat dry. *(Make-ahead: Refrigerate in airtight container for up to 24 hours.)*

In large bowl, toss together beans, rapini and dressing. Transfer to serving platter; sprinkle with almonds.

NUTRITIONAL INFORMATION, PER SERVING: about 116 cal, 3 g pro, 9 g total fat (1 g sat. fat), 8 g carb (3 g dietary fibre, 3 g sugar), 0 mg chol, 364 mg sodium, 245 mg potassium. % RDI: 8% calcium, 13% iron, 12% vit A, 22% vit C, 21% folate.

SERVING SUGGESTION

Serve **Potato Fennel Gratin** with **Lemon and Herb Spatchcock Chicken** (recipe, page 61) and **Sautéed Green Beans With Balsamic Shallots** (recipe, page 115)

Potato Fennel Gratin

HANDS-ON TIME	TOTAL TIME	MAKES
35 MINUTES	1 HOUR	8 TO 10 SERVINGS

What you need

GRATIN

4	strips bacon
1 tsp	olive oil
1	small bulb fennel, trimmed, cored and thinly sliced
2	carrots, thinly sliced on the diagonal
1.2 kg	yellow-fleshed potatoes (about 8), peeled and cut in ¼-inch (5 mm) thick slices
1½ cups	sodium-reduced chicken broth
1 cup	whipping cream (35%)
½ cup	milk
3	sprigs fresh thyme
2	cloves garlic, thinly sliced
½ tsp	each salt and pepper
3 tbsp	all-purpose flour
1 cup	shredded Gruyère cheese

TOPPING

1 cup	fresh bread crumbs
½ cup	shredded Gruyère cheese
2 tbsp	butter, melted

How to make it

GRATIN: In large nonstick skillet, cook bacon over medium-high heat, turning once, until crisp, about 4 minutes. Remove to paper towel–lined plate to drain. Chop bacon into ½-inch (1 cm) pieces. Set aside.

Reserving 2 tsp of the fat, drain pan. Return reserved fat to pan. Add oil; heat over medium-high heat. Cook fennel and carrots, stirring, just until fennel is softened, about 7 minutes. (If fennel begins to stick to pan, add water, 1 tbsp at a time.) Remove to plate.

In same pan, bring potatoes, broth, cream, milk, thyme, garlic, salt and pepper to boil over medium-high heat. Reduce heat to medium; simmer until potatoes are almost tender, about 10 minutes.

Whisk flour with ¼ cup water. Move potatoes to 1 side of pan; whisk flour mixture into liquid in pan until smooth. Add bacon and fennel mixture; cook, stirring, until potatoes are fork-tender, about 2 minutes. Discard thyme.

Spoon half of the potato mixture into greased 13- x 9-inch (3 L) baking dish; sprinkle with Gruyère. Scrape remaining potato mixture over top. (Make-ahead: Let cool completely; cover with foil. Refrigerate for up to 24 hours. Reheat, covered, on bottom rack of 425°F/220°C oven for 45 minutes before continuing with recipe.)

TOPPING: Stir together bread crumbs, Gruyère and butter. Sprinkle over potato mixture.

Bake on bottom rack of 425°F (220°C) oven until top is golden, about 15 minutes. Let stand for 10 minutes before serving.

NUTRITIONAL INFORMATION, PER EACH OF 10 SERVINGS: about 344 cal, 11 g pro, 21 g total fat (11 g sat. fat), 30 g carb (3 g dietary fibre, 4 g sugar), 62 mg chol, 460 mg sodium, 830 mg potassium. % RDI: 22% calcium, 11% iron, 61% vit A, 33% vit C, 15% folate.

Smooth and Creamy Mashed Potatoes

p.113

HANDS-ON TIME		TOTAL TIME		MAKES
15 MINUTES	•	30 MINUTES	•	8 TO 10 SERVINGS

What you need

2.25 kg	russet potatoes, peeled and cut in chunks
1¼ cups	10% cream
¼ cup	butter
1 tsp	salt
¼ tsp	pepper

How to make it

In large saucepan of boiling salted water, cook potatoes until fork-tender, about 15 minutes; drain well. Press potatoes through potato ricer. *(Make-ahead: Spread onto parchment paper–lined rimmed baking sheet; let cool. Cover and refrigerate for up to 24 hours. Continue with recipe, adding 8 minutes to cook time.)*

In large saucepan, heat together cream, butter, salt and pepper over medium heat until butter is melted. Add potatoes; cook, stirring frequently, until smooth and hot, about 4 minutes.

TIP FROM THE TEST KITCHEN

Russet potatoes, with their high starch content, make for fluffy, airy mashed potatoes as well as deliciously creamy baked potatoes. Cooking the potatoes for this mash recipe a day ahead saves time; simply stir together the ingredients and reheat 12 minutes before dinner.

NUTRITIONAL INFORMATION, PER EACH OF 10 SERVINGS:
about 226 cal, 5 g pro, 8 g total fat (5 g sat. fat), 36 g carb (2 g dietary fibre, 1 g sugar), 22 mg chol, 730 mg sodium, 751 mg potassium. % RDI: 5% calcium, 11% iron, 6% vit A, 47% vit C, 11% folate.

Grilled Baked Potatoes With Green Onion Sour Cream

 p.61

HANDS-ON TIME
20 MINUTES

TOTAL TIME
1¼ HOURS

MAKES
6 SERVINGS

What you need

POTATOES
3	large baking potatoes (such as russet)
1 tbsp	olive oil
pinch	salt

GREEN ONION SOUR CREAM
⅓ cup	sour cream
2	green onions, minced
¼ tsp	pepper

How to make it

POTATOES: Using fork, prick potatoes all over. Bake in 400°F (200°C) oven, turning once, until tender, 50 to 60 minutes. Set aside until cool enough to handle. *(Make-ahead: Let cool completely; refrigerate in airtight container for up to 3 days. Continue with recipe, adding 5 minutes to cook time.)*

Halve potatoes lengthwise; brush cut sides with oil and sprinkle with salt. Place, cut sides down, on greased grill over medium heat; grill, uncovered, turning once, until grill-marked, about 15 minutes.

GREEN ONION SOUR CREAM: While potatoes are cooking, in small bowl, stir together sour cream, green onions and pepper. *(Make-ahead: Refrigerate in airtight container for up to 3 days.)* Serve with potatoes.

TIP FROM THE TEST KITCHEN
Don't want to heat your oven? Bake the pricked potatoes on the indirect heat of your outdoor grill. Place on 1 rack of 2-burner barbecue or on centre rack of 3-burner barbecue. Heat adjacent burner(s) to medium-high heat; close lid and grill, turning potatoes once, until tender, 50 to 60 minutes.

NUTRITIONAL INFORMATION, PER SERVING: about 208 cal, 5 g pro, 4 g total fat (2 g sat. fat), 39 g carb (4 g dietary fibre, 2 g sugar), 4 mg chol, 27 mg sodium, 982 mg potassium. % RDI: 4% calcium, 14% iron, 2% vit A, 30% vit C, 25% folate.

Parsnip and Potato Purée

HANDS-ON TIME	TOTAL TIME	MAKES
25 MINUTES	35 MINUTES	10 TO 12 SERVINGS

What you need

900 g	parsnips, peeled, halved lengthwise and cut in 1-inch (2.5 cm) lengths
900 g	yellow-fleshed potatoes (about 6), peeled and cubed
3	cloves garlic, quartered
1 cup	buttermilk
2 tsp	Dijon mustard
½ tsp	salt
3 tbsp	chopped fresh chives

How to make it

In large saucepan of boiling salted water, cook parsnips, potatoes and garlic until tender, 10 to 12 minutes. Drain.

In food processor, in 2 batches, purée together parsnip mixture, buttermilk, mustard and salt just until smooth. *(Make-ahead: Let cool for 30 minutes; cover and refrigerate in airtight container for up to 2 days. Reheat to serve.)* Transfer to serving dish; stir in chives.

TIP FROM THE TEST KITCHEN
To avoid a gluey purée, don't overprocess the parsnip mixture.

NUTRITIONAL INFORMATION, PER EACH OF 12 SERVINGS:
about 112 cal, 3 g pro, 1 g total fat (trace sat. fat), 25 g carb (3 g dietary fibre, 5 g sugar), 2 mg chol, 434 mg sodium, 484 mg potassium. % RDI: 6% calcium, 4% iron, 1% vit A, 23% vit C, 24% folate.

Chestnut and Mushroom Stuffing

HANDS-ON TIME	•	TOTAL TIME	•	MAKES
30 MINUTES		30 MINUTES		12 TO 16 SERVINGS

What you need

2 tbsp	olive oil
3	cloves garlic, minced
1	rib celery, diced
1	onion, diced
675 g	sliced mixed mushrooms (such as oyster and cremini)
¼ cup	dry white wine
12 cups	cubed sourdough bread (about 1 loaf)
1 cup	peeled roasted chestnuts (about two 100 g bags), coarsely chopped
¼ cup	sodium-reduced chicken broth
¼ cup	water
¼ tsp	pepper
1 cup	grated Parmesan cheese
3 tbsp	chopped fresh parsley

How to make it

In Dutch oven or large skillet, heat oil over medium heat; cook garlic, celery and onion, stirring often, until onion is softened, about 5 minutes.

Add mushrooms; cook, stirring frequently, until tender and almost no liquid remains, about 8 minutes.

Add wine; cook, stirring, until reduced by half, about 1 minute. Stir in bread, chestnuts, broth, water and pepper. Remove from heat.

Stir in half of the Parmesan. Scrape into lightly greased 13- x 9-inch (3 L) baking dish. Sprinkle with remaining Parmesan. *(Make-ahead: Cover and refrigerate for up to 24 hours. Bake, covered, in 425°F/220°C oven until warmed through, about 15 minutes. Uncover and continue with recipe.)*

Bake in 425°F (220°C) oven until top is crisp, about 5 minutes. Sprinkle with parsley.

TIP FROM THE TEST KITCHEN
Chestnuts in the shell are time-consuming to boil and peel; instead, look for packages of ready-to-eat, peeled whole chestnuts in the grocery store.

NUTRITIONAL INFORMATION, PER EACH OF 16 SERVINGS:
about 150 cal, 7 g pro, 4 g total fat (1 g sat. fat), 21 g carb (2 g dietary fibre, 3 g sugar), 6 mg chol, 263 mg sodium, 303 mg potassium.
% RDI: 8% calcium, 10% iron, 2% vit A, 6% vit C, 32% folate.

Sausage, Apple and Sage Stuffing

HANDS-ON TIME	•	TOTAL TIME	•	MAKES
25 MINUTES		1 HOUR		8 TO 10 SERVINGS

What you need

12 cups	cubed crusty French or Italian bread (about 1 loaf)
¼ cup	butter
1	pkg (500 g) fresh pork sausage, casings removed
2 cups	diced leeks (white and light green parts only)
1 cup	diced celery
2	sweet cooking apples (such as Gala), peeled, cored and diced
½ tsp	pepper
¼ tsp	salt
⅓ cup	chopped fresh parsley
3 tbsp	chopped fresh sage
1½ cups	sodium-reduced chicken broth
2	eggs

How to make it

Arrange bread on rimmed baking sheet; toast in 350°F (180°C) oven until light golden, 10 to 12 minutes. Transfer to large bowl.

While bread is toasting, in large skillet, melt half of the butter over medium-high heat; cook sausage, breaking up with spoon, until browned, about 8 minutes. Using slotted spoon, remove to bowl with bread.

In same skillet, melt remaining butter over medium heat; cook leeks and celery, stirring occasionally, until beginning to soften, about 6 minutes. Add apples, pepper and salt; cook, stirring, until tender-crisp, about 4 minutes. Stir into bread mixture. Add parsley and sage.

In bowl, whisk broth with eggs; drizzle over bread mixture. Toss to coat.

Scrape into greased 13- x 9-inch (3 L) baking dish; cover with foil. *(Make-ahead: Refrigerate for up to 24 hours. Let stand at room temperature for 1 hour before continuing with recipe.)* Bake in 425°F (220°C) oven for 20 minutes; uncover and bake until top is browned, 10 to 15 minutes.

TIP FROM THE TEST KITCHEN

Switch up the flavour of this stuffing with different types of sausage, such as farmer's, honey-garlic or chorizo.

NUTRITIONAL INFORMATION, PER EACH OF 10 SERVINGS: about 345 cal, 14 g pro, 20 g total fat (8 g sat. fat), 28 g carb (2 g dietary fibre, 6 g sugar), 87 mg chol, 757 mg sodium, 293 mg potassium. % RDI: 5% calcium, 19% iron, 12% vit A, 10% vit C, 30% folate.

SERVING SUGGESTION

Serve this **Sausage, Apple and Sage Stuffing** with **Smooth and Creamy Mashed Potatoes** (recipe, page 108) and roast turkey for a traditional holiday meal.

Cider-Braised Red Cabbage

HANDS-ON TIME	•	TOTAL TIME	•	MAKES
35 MINUTES		1¼ HOURS		10 SERVINGS

What you need

¼ cup	butter
4	strips thick-cut bacon, cut crosswise in ¼-inch (5 mm) thick slices
1	sweet onion, thinly sliced
1	red cabbage (about 1.35 kg), thinly sliced
1	Granny Smith apple, peeled and thinly sliced
¼ cup	dry hard cider
2 tbsp	cider vinegar
1 tsp	mustard seeds
½ tsp	each salt and pepper

How to make it

In Dutch oven or large heavy-bottomed saucepan, melt butter over medium-high heat; cook bacon until fat begins to render, about 2 minutes.

Add onion; cook, stirring occasionally, until bacon is crisp and onion is softened, 8 to 10 minutes.

Add cabbage, apple, cider, vinegar, mustard seeds, salt and pepper; cook over medium heat until cabbage is slightly wilted, 5 to 7 minutes.

Cover and reduce heat to low; cook, stirring occasionally, until apple and cabbage are tender and almost no liquid remains, 40 to 50 minutes. *(Make-ahead: Let cool; refrigerate in airtight container for up to 2 days. Reheat over medium heat, about 10 minutes.)*

TIP FROM THE TEST KITCHEN

You can replace hard cider (which contains alcohol) with a late-harvest wine or regular apple cider; just add an extra 1 tbsp cider vinegar to the recipe.

NUTRITIONAL INFORMATION, PER SERVING: about 135 cal, 3 g pro, 10 g total fat (6 g sat. fat), 9 g carb (2 g dietary fibre), 20 mg chol, 229 mg sodium, 181 mg potassium. % RDI: 4% calcium, 3% iron, 5% vit A, 38% vit C, 13% folate.

Sautéed Green Beans With Balsamic Shallots

p.106

HANDS-ON TIME	TOTAL TIME	MAKES
25 MINUTES	25 MINUTES	8 SERVINGS

What you need

3 tbsp	butter
500 g	shallots, quartered
½ tsp	each salt and pepper
¼ cup	balsamic vinegar
2 tsp	granulated sugar
675 g	green beans, trimmed

How to make it

In large skillet, melt half of the butter over medium heat; cook shallots and 1 pinch each of the salt and pepper, stirring occasionally and adding water, 1 tbsp at a time, if shallots begin to stick to pan, until softened and golden, about 15 minutes.

Add vinegar and sugar; cook, stirring, until thickened and shallots are coated, about 5 minutes. *(Make-ahead: Let cool; refrigerate in airtight container for up to 2 days.)*

Meanwhile, in large saucepan of boiling salted water, cook green beans until tender-crisp, about 2 minutes; drain. *(Make-ahead: Transfer to large bowl of ice water; drain. Refrigerate in resealable bag for up to 2 days. Continue with recipe as directed, adding 2 minutes to cook time.)*

In separate large skillet, melt remaining butter over medium-high heat; cook green beans and remaining salt and pepper, stirring, just until tender, about 1 minute. Stir in shallots until heated through.

TIP FROM THE TEST KITCHEN
When trimming the shallots, cut away only the tip of the root ends; the rest of the root will help keep each shallot intact as it cooks.

NUTRITIONAL INFORMATION, PER SERVING: about 113 cal, 3 g pro, 5 g total fat (3 g sat. fat), 17 g carb (3 g dietary fibre, 5 g sugar), 11 mg chol, 183 mg sodium, 297 mg potassium. % RDI: 5% calcium, 9% iron, 14% vit A, 12% vit C, 17% folate.

Grilled Peppers and Onions

HANDS-ON TIME
15 MINUTES

TOTAL TIME
15 MINUTES

MAKES
6 SERVINGS

What you need

2	red onions
2	sweet red peppers
2	sweet yellow peppers
4 tsp	olive oil
¼ tsp	each salt and pepper

How to make it

Slice red onions crosswise into ½-inch (1 cm) thick rounds. Slice red peppers and yellow peppers crosswise into ½-inch (1 cm) thick rings; remove seeds and trim white veins.

Thread red onions onto metal or soaked wooden skewers; brush with half of the oil and sprinkle with half each of the salt and pepper. Toss together red peppers, yellow peppers and remaining oil, salt and pepper.

Place red onion skewers, red peppers and yellow peppers on greased grill over medium-high heat; close lid and grill, turning occasionally, until tender and grill-marked, 10 to 15 minutes. *(Make-ahead: Refrigerate in airtight container for up to 3 days. Reheat before serving.)*

TIP FROM THE TEST KITCHEN
Threading onion slices onto skewers, lollipop-style, helps prevent smaller rings from falling through the cooking grate; if you thread them through two skewers, they won't spin when you flip them.

NUTRITIONAL INFORMATION, PER SERVING: about 98 cal, 2 g pro, 3 g total fat (trace sat. fat), 17 g carb (3 g dietary fibre, 8 g sugar), 0 mg chol, 101 mg sodium, 374 mg potassium. % RDI: 3% calcium, 6% iron, 19% vit A, 330% vit C, 15% folate.

SERVING SUGGESTION

Try these **Grilled Peppers and Onions** with **Creamy Tortellini Salad** (recipe, page 103) and your favourite grilled sausages.

Grilled Harvest Vegetables

HANDS-ON TIME
30 MINUTES

•

TOTAL TIME
1½ HOURS

•

MAKES
ABOUT 12 CUPS

What you need

3	sweet red peppers
3	sweet yellow peppers
2	zucchini
2	red onions
1	eggplant (about 450 g)
½ tsp	salt
⅓ cup	olive oil
1	clove garlic, minced
¼ tsp	each salt, pepper and hot pepper flakes

How to make it

Quarter red peppers and yellow peppers; remove seeds and cores. Trim ends off zucchini; cut lengthwise into ¼-inch (5 mm) thick strips. Cut onions into ¼-inch (5 mm) thick rings. Cut eggplant crosswise into ½-inch (1 cm) thick slices.

Thread onions onto metal or soaked wooden skewers. Place eggplant in colander; sprinkle both sides with salt. Let stand for 30 minutes; pat dry.

Whisk together oil, garlic, salt, pepper and hot pepper flakes; brush over vegetables.

Working in batches if necessary, place peppers on greased grill over medium-high heat; close lid and grill, turning once, until grill-marked and tender, 15 to 20 minutes. Remove and let cool enough to handle; coarsely chop.

Repeat with zucchini, onions and eggplant, grilling for about 8 minutes.

Toss together peppers, zucchini, onions and eggplant. *(Make-ahead: Refrigerate in airtight container for up to 3 days.)*

TIP FROM THE TEST KITCHEN

Grill vegetables ahead of time and you have the makings of many easy meals. Use them in sandwiches and burgers, toss with pasta or fold into frittatas and omelettes.

NUTRITIONAL INFORMATION, PER 1 CUP: about 107 cal, 2 g pro, 6 g total fat (1 g sat. fat), 13 g carb (3 g dietary fibre), 0 mg chol, 99 mg sodium, 298 mg potassium. % RDI: 2% calcium, 4% iron, 15% vit A, 158% vit C, 13% folate.

Quick Cabbage Kimchi

HANDS-ON TIME		TOTAL TIME		MAKES
1¾ HOURS	•	5¼ HOURS	•	ABOUT 8 CUPS

What you need

How to make it

SALTED CABBAGE
1 head	napa cabbage (about 900 g)
¼ cup	Korean fine sea salt

VEGETABLES
3 cups	diagonally sliced mini cucumbers
½ cup	thinly sliced onion
⅓ cup	diagonally sliced carrot
2 tbsp	Korean coarse red pepper powder
2 tbsp	granulated sugar
2 tsp	Korean fine sea salt

SPICE PASTE
2	long red hot peppers, chopped
1	Thai bird's-eye pepper, chopped
3 tbsp	chopped garlic
4 tsp	rice vinegar or white vinegar
2 tsp	chopped fresh ginger
1 tbsp	fish sauce
1½ tsp	minced salted shrimp
4	green onions
1 tbsp	toasted sesame seeds

SALTED CABBAGE: Discard outer green leaves of cabbage; separate remaining leaves from core. Halve leaves lengthwise; cut diagonally into 1-inch (2.5 cm) wide strips. In large wide bowl, layer one-quarter of the leaves, 1 tbsp of the salt and 2 tbsp water. Repeat layers 3 times.

Sprinkle with an additional ½ cup water. Let stand until leaves are softened, at least 1 hour, turning over every 20 minutes. Drain and immerse in cold water; repeat once. Drain in colander for 15 minutes. Return to bowl.

VEGETABLES: Add cucumbers, onion and carrot to cabbage; sprinkle with red pepper powder, sugar and salt. Set aside.

SPICE PASTE: In food processor, purée together long red hot peppers, Thai bird's-eye pepper, garlic, vinegar, ginger and fish sauce until smooth, about 20 seconds; add to cabbage mixture. With wooden spoon or wearing rubber gloves, mix well. Stir in shrimp.

Halve green onions lengthwise; diagonally cut into 1-inch (2.5 cm) pieces. Stir onions and sesame seeds into cabbage mixture util combined. Cover and refrigerate for at least 3 hours. (*Make-ahead: Refrigerate for up to 5 days.*)

TIP FROM THE TEST KITCHEN
Look for salted shrimp, a Korean specialty, in Asian grocery stores.

NUTRITIONAL INFORMATION, PER ¼ CUP: about 17 cal, 1 g pro, trace total fat (trace sat. fat), 3 g carb (1 g dietary fibre), 1 mg chol, 623 mg sodium, 117 mg potassium. % RDI: 3% calcium, 2% iron, 4% vit A, 22% vit C, 12% folate.

Pumpkin Cheesecake
With White Chocolate Almond Bark

HANDS-ON TIME	•	TOTAL TIME	•	MAKES
45 MINUTES		8¾ HOURS		12 SERVINGS

What you need

PUMPKIN CHEESECAKE

1 cup	pumpkin purée
1 cup	English-style gingersnap cookie crumbs (2 cups whole cookies)
½ cup	ground almonds
1¼ cups	granulated sugar
3 tbsp	butter, melted
2	pkg (each 250 g) cream cheese, softened
3	eggs
2 tsp	each cinnamon and ground ginger
1 tsp	vanilla
½ tsp	nutmeg
pinch	each ground cloves and salt
3 cups	sour cream
1 cup	whipping cream (35%)

WHITE CHOCOLATE ALMOND BARK

170 g	white chocolate (6 oz), melted
⅓ cup	sliced natural (skin-on) almonds, toasted

How to make it

PUMPKIN CHEESECAKE: Scrape pumpkin purée into centre of a square of cheesecloth; wrap in a bundle, twisting top to seal. Place bundle in colander set over bowl. Place small plate and a heavy can (to help press liquids from purée) on top of bundle. Let drain for 1½ hours; discard liquid.

In bowl, stir together gingersnap crumbs, ground almonds, ¼ cup of the sugar and the butter until moistened. Scrape mixture into greased 9-inch (2.5 L) springform pan; press into bottom and about ¾ inch (2 cm) up side of pan. Bake in 350°F (180°C) oven until set, 12 to 15 minutes. Let cool.

In large bowl, beat cream cheese until smooth. Gradually beat in remaining sugar, scraping down side of bowl twice, until light and smooth, about 3 minutes. On low speed, beat in eggs, 1 at a time, scraping down side of bowl often, just until smooth. Beat in pumpkin purée, cinnamon, ginger, vanilla, nutmeg, cloves and salt. Beat in sour cream. Pour over crust, smoothing top.

Bake on rimmed baking sheet in 300°F (150°C) oven until top is no longer shiny and edge is set yet centre still jiggles slightly, 2 to 2¼ hours.

Turn off oven; run knife around edge of cake. Let cool in oven for 1 hour. Transfer to rack; let cool completely. Refrigerate until chilled, at least 4 hours. *(Make-ahead: Cover and refrigerate for up to 2 days or wrap in heavy-duty foil and freeze for up to 2 weeks.)*

Whip cream until stiff peaks form; spread over top of cheesecake.

WHITE CHOCOLATE ALMOND BARK: On parchment paper–lined baking sheet, spread all but 3 tbsp of the chocolate in 1/16-inch (2 mm) thick layer. Sprinkle almonds evenly over top; drizzle with remaining chocolate. Refrigerate until firm, about 15 minutes. *(Make-ahead: Cover with plastic wrap; refrigerate for up to 24 hours.)* Break into 2-inch (5 cm) chunks. Arrange over top of cheesecake.

NUTRITIONAL INFORMATION, PER SERVING: about 613 cal, 12 g pro, 43 g total fat (23 g sat. fat), 49 g carb (2 g dietary fibre, 35 g sugar), 146 mg chol, 317 mg sodium, 392 mg potassium. % RDI: 19% calcium, 14% iron, 59% vit A, 2% vit C, 15% folate.

Slow Cooker Mini Orange and Ginger Cheesecakes

HANDS-ON TIME
30 MINUTES

TOTAL TIME
6½ HOURS

MAKES
6 SERVINGS

What you need

CRUST
⅔ cup	gingersnap cookie crumbs (8 to 10 cookies)
1 tbsp	packed brown sugar
1 tbsp	butter, melted
1½ tsp	minced crystallized ginger
pinch	cinnamon

FILLING
1	pkg (250 g) cream cheese, softened
1 tsp	cornstarch
⅓ cup	granulated sugar
1	egg
¼ cup	sour cream
1½ tsp	grated orange zest
1 tbsp	orange juice
½ tsp	vanilla
pinch	salt

GARNISH
½ cup	whipping cream (35%)
1 tsp	granulated sugar
	Orange zest, fresh mint leaves and/or minced crystallized ginger

How to make it

CRUST: Stir together cookie crumbs, brown sugar, butter, ginger and cinnamon until moistened; press scant 2 tbsp into each of 6 sterilized ½-cup (125 mL) canning jars or other small heatproof containers. Refrigerate until needed.

FILLING: In large bowl, beat cream cheese with cornstarch until smooth. Gradually beat in sugar until light and fluffy, scraping down side of bowl. Beat in egg just until combined. Beat in sour cream, orange zest, orange juice, vanilla and salt. Spoon over crusts.

Fill 6- to 7-quart (6 to 7 L) slow cooker with enough hot water to come ½-inch (1 cm) up sides. Arrange jars, uncovered and not touching, in slow cooker. Cover with 4 layers of paper towels; secure with slow cooker lid. Cook on low until no longer shiny and edges are set yet centres still jiggle slightly, about 1½ hours. Using canning tongs, remove jars to rack; let cool.

Cover and refrigerate until chilled, about 4 hours. *(Make-ahead: Refrigerate for up to 2 days.)*

GARNISH: Beat cream with sugar until soft peaks form; spoon over cheesecakes. Top with orange zest, mint leaves and/or ginger as desired.

TIP FROM THE TEST KITCHEN
The layer of paper towels keeps the moist heat in while preventing condensation from dripping onto the cakes.

NUTRITIONAL INFORMATION, PER SERVING: about 390 cal, 6 g pro, 27 g total fat (16 g sat. fat), 32 g carb (1 g dietary fibre, 19 g sugar), 111 mg chol, 273 mg sodium, 202 mg potassium. % RDI: 7% calcium, 14% iron, 28% vit A, 7% vit C, 11% folate.

Classic Chocolate Layer Cake

HANDS-ON TIME
45 MINUTES

TOTAL TIME
2½ HOURS

MAKES
12 TO 16 SERVINGS

What you need

CAKE

3 cups	all-purpose flour
2 cups	granulated sugar
⅔ cup	cocoa powder, sifted
2 tsp	baking soda
½ tsp	salt
2 cups	cooled brewed coffee or water
1 cup	vegetable oil
2 tsp	vanilla
3 tbsp	cider vinegar

CHOCOLATE ICING

2 cups	unsalted butter, softened
⅔ cup	whipping cream (35%)
4 tsp	vanilla
¼ tsp	salt
5 cups	icing sugar
225 g	unsweetened chocolate (8 oz), melted and cooled

How to make it

CAKE: Grease two 9-inch (1.5 L) round cake pans; line bottoms with parchment paper. Set aside. In large bowl, whisk together flour, sugar, cocoa powder, baking soda and salt. Whisk in coffee, oil and vanilla. Stir in vinegar. Scrape into prepared pans. Bake in 350°F (180°C) oven until cake tester inserted in centres comes out clean, 25 to 30 minutes. Let cool in pans on racks for 10 minutes. Invert onto racks; peel off paper. Let cool completely. *(Make-ahead: Store in airtight container for up to 24 hours.)*

CHOCOLATE ICING: In bowl, beat butter until light and fluffy; beat in cream, vanilla and salt. Beat in sugar, 1 cup at a time, until smooth; beat in chocolate, scraping down side of bowl often, until fluffy, about 2 minutes.

ASSEMBLY: Slice each cake in half horizontally to make 4 layers. Place 1 layer, cut side up, on cake plate; slide strips of waxed paper between cake and plate. Spread about ¾ cup of the icing over cut side; top with 1 of the remaining layers, cut side down. Spread about ¾ cup of the remaining icing over top of second layer. Repeat with remaining cake layers and icing, omitting icing from top of stack. Using large offset palette knife, spread about 1 cup of the remaining icing all over cake to seal in crumbs; refrigerate until firm, about 30 minutes.

Using palette knife, spread remaining icing all over cake, smoothing sides and top. Run tip of palette knife back and forth loosely across top to form gentle ripples, if desired. Remove waxed paper strips. *(Make-ahead: Refrigerate until firm, about 1 hour. Cover loosely with plastic wrap and refrigerate for up to 24 hours.)*

NUTRITIONAL INFORMATION, PER EACH OF 16 SERVINGS:
about 760 cal, 6 g pro, 48 g total fat (23 g sat. fat), 86 g carb (4 g dietary fibre), 73 mg chol, 242 mg sodium, 263 mg potassium. % RDI: 3% calcium, 30% iron, 24% vit A, 19% folate.

The Ultimate Carrot Layer Cake

HANDS-ON TIME		TOTAL TIME		MAKES
1 HOUR	•	4 HOURS	•	16 SERVINGS

What you need

CAKE
2 cups	all-purpose flour
2 tsp	baking powder
2 tsp	cinnamon
1 tsp	baking soda
¾ tsp	salt
½ tsp	nutmeg
3	eggs
¾ cup	granulated sugar
¾ cup	packed brown sugar
¾ cup	vegetable oil
1 tsp	vanilla
2 cups	grated carrots (about 2 large)
1	can (398 mL) crushed pineapple, drained
½ cup	chopped pecans

CREAM CHEESE ICING
2	pkg (each 250 g) cream cheese, softened
½ cup	butter, softened
1 tsp	vanilla
6 cups	icing sugar

How to make it

CAKE: In large bowl, whisk together flour, baking powder, cinnamon, baking soda, salt and nutmeg. In separate bowl, beat together eggs, granulated sugar, brown sugar, oil and vanilla until smooth; stir into flour mixture just until moistened. Stir in carrots, pineapple and pecans until combined. Scrape into 2 greased and floured 8-inch (1.2 L) round cake pans. Bake in 350°F (180°C) oven until cake tester inserted in centres comes out clean, 35 to 38 minutes. Let cool in pans on rack. (*Make-ahead: Cover with plastic wrap and store at room temperature for up to 2 days, or overwrap with heavy-duty foil and freeze for up to 2 weeks; thaw before continuing with recipe.*)

CREAM CHEESE ICING: In bowl, beat cream cheese with butter until smooth. Beat in vanilla. Beat in icing sugar, one-third at a time, until smooth and combined.

ASSEMBLY: Slice each cake in half horizontally to make 4 layers. Place 1 layer, cut side up, on cake plate; slide strips of waxed paper between cake and plate. Spread about ¾ cup of the icing over cut side; top with 1 of the remaining layers, cut side down. Spread about ¾ cup of the remaining icing over top of second layer. Repeat with remaining cake layers and icing, omitting icing from top of stack. Using large offset palette knife, spread thin layer of the remaining icing all over cake to seal in crumbs; refrigerate until firm, about 30 minutes.

Using palette knife, spread remaining icing all over cake. Remove waxed paper strips. Refrigerate for 30 minutes before serving. (*Make-ahead: Cover loosely and refrigerate for up to 24 hours.*)

VARIATION
The Ultimate Carrot Slab Cake
Prepare batter as directed; scrape into greased and floured 13- x 9-inch (3.5 L) cake pan. Bake until cake tester inserted in centre comes out clean, about 40 minutes. Let cool in pan on rack. Top with a half-batch of Cream Cheese Icing.

NUTRITIONAL INFORMATION, PER SERVING: about 611 cal, 5 g pro, 31 g total fat (11 g sat. fat), 82 g carb (2 g dietary fibre, 68 g sugar), 84 mg chol, 389 mg sodium, 157 mg potassium. % RDI: 7% calcium, 10% iron, 40% vit A, 2% vit C, 16% folate.

Buttery Pound Cake With Orange Chocolate Sauce

HANDS-ON TIME	•	TOTAL TIME	•	MAKES
25 MINUTES		2¾ HOURS		16 SERVINGS

What you need

POUND CAKE

1 cup	unsalted butter, softened
1¼ cups	granulated sugar
4	eggs, room temperature
3 tbsp	milk, room temperature
1 tbsp	vanilla
½ tsp	salt
1¾ cups	all-purpose flour, sifted

ORANGE CHOCOLATE SAUCE

⅔ cup	each cocoa powder and corn syrup
3 strips	orange zest
225 g	semisweet chocolate (about 8 oz), chopped
3 tbsp	orange-flavoured liqueur, such as Grand Marnier
pinch	salt

How to make it

POUND CAKE: In large bowl, beat butter with sugar until light, fluffy and pale yellow, about 5 minutes. Add 1 egg; beat for 2 minutes, scraping down side. Repeat with remaining eggs, adding 1 at a time. Beat in milk, vanilla and salt until combined (mixture may appear curdled).

Add half of the flour; stir gently just until combined. Repeat with remaining flour. Scrape into parchment paper–lined 8- x 4-inch (1.5 L) loaf pan, smoothing top.

Bake in 325°F (160°C) oven until top is golden and cake tester inserted in centre comes out clean, about 1¼ hours. Let cool in pan for 20 minutes. Turn out onto rack; let cool completely. Peel off parchment paper. *(Make-ahead: Wrap in plastic wrap; store for up to 2 days.)*

ORANGE CHOCOLATE SAUCE: Sift cocoa powder. In saucepan, bring cocoa powder, corn syrup, orange zest and 1 cup water to boil. Reduce heat to medium; boil, whisking constantly, for 2 minutes. Reduce heat to low; discard orange zest. Add chocolate and orange liqueur; cook, whisking constantly, until chocolate is melted, about 2 minutes. Remove from heat; whisk in salt. *(Make-ahead: Let cool for 30 minutes; refrigerate in airtight container for up to 7 days. Reheat to room temperature before serving.)*

TIP FROM THE TEST KITCHEN
A true pound cake batter contains no baking powder for leavening; it relies on beating each egg thoroughly.

NUTRITIONAL INFORMATION, PER SERVING: about 355 cal, 6 g pro, 18 g total fat (10.5 g sat. fat), 48.5 g carb (2.5 g dietary fibre, 29 g sugar), 76 mg chol, 110 mg sodium, 178 mg potassium. % RDI: 1% calcium, 14% iron, 13% vit A, 12% folate.

Double-Chocolate Zucchini Bundt Cake

HANDS-ON TIME	•	TOTAL TIME	•	MAKES
30 MINUTES		2¾ HOURS		12 SERVINGS

What you need

How to make it

CAKE
1 cup	butter, softened
1⅓ cups	packed brown sugar
3	eggs
¾ cup	milk
¾ cup	vegetable oil
2½ cups	all-purpose flour
1 tbsp	baking powder
¾ tsp	each baking soda and salt
¾ cup	cocoa powder
2½ cups	grated zucchini (peel-on)
1 cup	semisweet chocolate chips

CHOCOLATE SAUCE
170 g	bittersweet chocolate (about 6 oz), chopped
⅓ cup	whipping cream (35%)
2 tbsp	corn syrup

CAKE: In large bowl, beat butter with brown sugar until fluffy. Beat in eggs, 1 at a time, until combined. Beat in milk and oil.

In separate bowl, whisk together flour, baking powder, baking soda and salt; sift in cocoa powder.

Stir flour mixture into butter mixture just until combined. Fold in zucchini and chocolate chips. Scrape into greased and floured 10-cup (2.5 L) Bundt pan, smoothing top.

Bake in 325°F (160°C) oven until cake tester inserted in centre comes out clean, about 1¼ hours. Let cool in pan for 10 minutes. Using tip of knife, loosen edge of cake from pan. Invert rack over pan; turn cake out onto rack and remove pan. Slide sheet of foil or waxed paper under rack (to keep work surface clean). Let cool completely. *(Make-ahead: Wrap in plastic wrap and store for up to 2 days or freeze in airtight container for up to 2 weeks.)*

CHOCOLATE SAUCE: While cake is cooling, in heatproof bowl set over saucepan of hot (not boiling) water, heat together chocolate, cream and corn syrup, stirring, until melted and smooth, about 5 minutes.

Let cool until lukewarm and sauce runs slowly off back of spoon, about 15 minutes. Spoon or spread over top of cake.

TIP FROM THE TEST KITCHEN
Greasing your Bundt pan with butter and then dusting with flour ensures your cake will come out easily.

NUTRITIONAL INFORMATION, PER SERVING: about 672 cal, 8 g pro, 44 g total fat (19 g sat. fat), 67 g carb (5 g dietary fibre, 40 g sugar), 99 mg chol, 448 mg sodium, 433 mg potassium. % RDI: 10% calcium, 28% iron, 21% vit A, 5% vit C, 25% folate.

Maple-Glazed Doughnut Bundt Cake

HANDS-ON TIME
30 MINUTES

TOTAL TIME
2½ HOURS

MAKES
12 TO 16 SERVINGS

What you need

CAKE
1 cup	butter, softened
1½ cups	granulated sugar
4	eggs, separated
¼ cup	sour cream
1½ tsp	maple extract
3 cups	all-purpose flour
2 tsp	baking powder
½ tsp	salt
¼ tsp	baking soda
1 cup	buttermilk
3 tbsp	maple syrup
1 tbsp	warm water

MAPLE GLAZE
3 tbsp	maple syrup
1 tsp	maple extract
1 cup	icing sugar

How to make it

CAKE: In large bowl, beat butter with 1 cup of the sugar until fluffy. Beat in egg yolks, 1 at a time. Beat in sour cream and maple extract. In separate bowl, whisk together flour, baking powder, salt and baking soda. Stir into butter mixture, alternating with buttermilk, making 3 additions of flour mixture and 2 of buttermilk, to make stiff batter.

In separate bowl, using clean beaters, beat egg whites until soft peaks form. Beat in remaining sugar, 1 tbsp at a time, until firm glossy peaks form. Fold one-third of the egg white mixture into batter to lighten it; fold in remaining egg white mixture. Scrape into greased and floured 10-inch (3 L) Bundt pan, smoothing top.

Bake in 350°F (180°C) oven until cake tester inserted in centre comes out clean, 40 to 50 minutes. Let cool in pan for 20 minutes. Using tip of knife, loosen edge of cake from pan. Invert rack over pan; turn cake out onto rack and remove pan.

Slide sheet of foil or waxed paper under rack (to keep work surface clean). Mix maple syrup with warm water; brush all over cake. Let cool completely.

MAPLE GLAZE: In bowl, mix maple syrup with maple extract; stir in icing sugar to make thick pourable glaze, adding up to ½ tsp water, a little at a time, to reach desired consistency. Pour over cake. Let stand until set, about 15 minutes. (*Make-ahead: Store in airtight container for up to 24 hours.*)

NUTRITIONAL INFORMATION, PER EACH OF 16 SERVINGS:
about 343 cal, 5 g pro, 14 g total fat (8 g sat. fat), 49 g carb (1 g dietary fibre, 31 g sugar), 81 mg chol, 244 mg sodium, 94 mg potassium. % RDI: 6% calcium, 10% iron, 13% vit A, 20% folate.

Slow Cooker Citrus Poppy Seed Cake

HANDS-ON TIME
35 MINUTES

•

TOTAL TIME
4 HOURS

•

MAKES
12 TO 16 SERVINGS

What you need

How to make it

CAKE

¼ cup	butter, softened
1½ cups	granulated sugar
¼ cup	vegetable oil
2	eggs
1 tbsp	grated lemon zest
1 tbsp	grated orange zest
2 tbsp	lemon juice
1 tsp	vanilla
2 cups	all-purpose flour
2 tbsp	poppy seeds
1 tsp	each baking powder and baking soda
½ tsp	salt
½ cup	each buttermilk and plain yogurt

CITRUS GLAZE

¾ cup	icing sugar
1 tsp	grated lemon zest
2 tbsp	lemon juice or orange juice

CAKE: Place insert of 5- to 6-quart (5 to 6 L) oval slow cooker on sheet of parchment paper. Adding 2 inches (5 cm) all around, trace around bottom; cut out shape. Grease insert; line with parchment paper cutout.

In large bowl, beat together butter, sugar and oil until fluffy. Beat in eggs, 1 at a time, beating well after each addition. Beat in lemon zest, orange zest, lemon juice and vanilla.

In separate bowl, whisk together flour, poppy seeds, baking powder, baking soda and salt. Stir into butter mixture, alternating with buttermilk and yogurt, making 3 additions of flour mixture and 2 of buttermilk and yogurt. Scrape into prepared slow cooker, smoothing top. Cover and cook on high until cake tester inserted in centre comes out clean, about 2 hours. Turn off slow cooker; uncover.

CITRUS GLAZE: Whisk together icing sugar, lemon zest and lemon juice until smooth; brush over hot cake. Let cool, uncovered, in slow cooker for 15 minutes.

Using parchment paper, lift out cake onto rack; let cool completely. *(Make-ahead: Store in airtight container for up to 2 days.)*

TIP FROM THE TEST KITCHEN
An oval slow cooker will give your cake the best height and shape.

NUTRITIONAL INFORMATION, PER EACH OF 16 SERVINGS:
about 234 cal, 3 g pro, 8 g total fat (3 g sat. fat), 38 g carb (1 g dietary fibre, 25 g sugar), 32 mg chol, 209 mg sodium, 72 mg potassium. % RDI: 5% calcium, 6% iron, 4% vit A, 5% vit C, 17% folate.

Lemon Coconut Tart

| HANDS-ON TIME | • | TOTAL TIME | • | MAKES |
| 30 MINUTES | | 4½ HOURS | | 8 SERVINGS |

What you need

How to make it

LEMON COCONUT CURD

4	eggs
4	egg yolks
¾ cup	granulated sugar
⅓ cup	coconut milk
1 tsp	grated lemon zest
½ cup	lemon juice
4 tsp	potato starch

COCONUT CRUST

⅔ cup	sweetened shredded coconut, toasted
¾ cup	ground almonds
½ cup	granulated sugar
6 tbsp	kosher pareve margarine, cubed
¾ tsp	ground ginger

LEMON COCONUT CURD: In heatproof bowl set over saucepan of gently simmering water, whisk together eggs, egg yolks, sugar, coconut milk, lemon zest and lemon juice. Whisk in potato starch.

Cook, whisking, until mixture is translucent and thick enough to mound on spoon, about 8 minutes. Strain into bowl; place plastic wrap directly on surface. Refrigerate until chilled, about 4 hours. (*Make-ahead: Refrigerate for up to 24 hours.*)

COCONUT CRUST: Set aside 2 tbsp of the coconut. In food processor, pulse together remaining coconut, the almonds, sugar, margarine and ginger until mixture begins to form small clumps. Press onto bottom and up side of lightly greased 9-inch (23 cm) round tart pan with removable bottom; refrigerate until firm, about 20 minutes.

Bake on baking sheet in 350°F (180°C) oven until golden, about 25 minutes. Let cool completely in pan on rack. (*Make-ahead: Cover and store in cool, dry place for up to 24 hours.*)

Spoon lemon mixture into crust; sprinkle with reserved coconut.

TIP FROM THE TEST KITCHEN
This tangy lemon tart is dairy- and gluten-free; coconut milk gives the lemon curd a rich flavour without requiring any butter.

NUTRITIONAL INFORMATION, PER SERVING: about 324 cal, 7 g pro, 17 g total fat (6 g sat. fat), 40 g carb (2 g dietary fibre, 36 g sugar), 188 mg chol, 139 mg sodium, 173 mg potassium. % RDI: 4% calcium, 11% iron, 20% vit A, 12% vit C, 15% folate.

Brûlée Lemon Tart

HANDS-ON TIME	•	TOTAL TIME	•	MAKES
55 MINUTES		7½ HOURS		8 TO 10 SERVINGS

What you need

FILLING

5	eggs
5	egg yolks
1 cup	granulated sugar
2 tsp	grated lemon zest
¾ cup	lemon juice
pinch	salt
2 tbsp	cold butter

PASTRY

1 cup	all-purpose flour
2 tbsp	granulated sugar
½ cup	cold butter, cubed
1	egg yolk
2 tbsp	ice water

TOPPING

2 tbsp	granulated sugar

How to make it

FILLING: In top of double boiler or large heatproof bowl set over saucepan of simmering water, whisk together eggs, egg yolks, sugar, lemon zest, lemon juice and salt; cook, stirring, until mixture is translucent and thick enough to mound on spoon, 10 to 15 minutes. Strain through fine-mesh sieve into bowl; stir in butter until melted. Place plastic wrap directly on surface. Refrigerate until chilled, about 2 hours. (*Make-ahead: Refrigerate for up to 24 hours.*)

PASTRY: While filling is chilling, in bowl, whisk flour with sugar. Using pastry blender or 2 knives, cut in butter until mixture resembles fine crumbs with a few larger pieces. Whisk egg yolk with ice water; drizzle over flour mixture, tossing with fork to form ragged dough. Shape into disc; wrap in plastic wrap. Let stand for 15 minutes.

On lightly floured work surface, roll out dough into 11-inch (28 cm) wide circle; fit into fluted 9-inch (23 cm) tart pan with removable bottom. Trim to fit, leaving 1-inch (2.5 cm) overhang; fold overhang inside pan and press to seal pastry. Refrigerate until firm, about 45 minutes. (*Make-ahead: Cover and refrigerate for up to 24 hours.*)

Prick bottom of crust at ½-inch (1 cm) intervals. Line with foil; fill with pie weights or dried beans. Bake on bottom rack of 400°F (200°C) oven until edge is golden, 12 to 15 minutes. Remove pie weights and foil; bake until crust is golden, 8 to 10 minutes. Let cool slightly on rack.

Spoon filling into crust, smoothing top. Bake on bottom rack of 325°F (160°C) oven until filling is set yet centre still jiggles slightly, 12 to 15 minutes. Let cool on rack for 30 minutes. Refrigerate until chilled, about 4 hours.

TOPPING: Sprinkle sugar evenly over top, leaving ½-inch (1 cm) border. Let stand for 5 minutes. Using blowtorch and holding flame at least ½ inch (1 cm) from surface, move flame back and forth over sugar until bubbling and dark amber. Let stand for 5 minutes before serving.

NUTRITIONAL INFORMATION, PER EACH OF 10 SERVINGS: about 322 cal, 6 g pro, 18 g total fat (9 g sat. fat), 36 g carb (trace dietary fibre, 26 g sugar), 242 mg chol, 119 mg sodium, 79 mg potassium. % RDI: 3% calcium, 10% iron, 21% vit A, 13% vit C, 24% folate.

Jam Streusel Mini Tarts

HANDS-ON TIME
35 MINUTES

TOTAL TIME
3 HOURS

MAKES
12 MINI TARTS

What you need

PASTRY
1¼ cups	all-purpose flour
¼ tsp	salt
¼ cup	cold butter, cubed
¼ cup	lard, cubed
2 tbsp	ice water (approx)
4 tsp	sour cream

ALMOND STREUSEL
½ cup	all-purpose flour
½ cup	granulated sugar
¼ cup	cold butter, cubed
⅓ cup	sliced natural (skin-on) almonds
1¼ cups	cherry jam

How to make it

PASTRY: In large bowl, whisk flour with salt. Using pastry blender or 2 knives, cut in butter and lard until mixture resembles coarse crumbs with a few larger pieces. Whisk ice water with sour cream; drizzle over flour mixture, tossing with fork to form ragged dough and adding up to 1 tsp more ice water if necessary. Shape into disc; wrap in plastic wrap. Refrigerate until chilled, about 1 hour.

On lightly floured work surface, roll out dough to ⅛-inch (3 mm) thickness. Using 3¾-inch (10 cm) round cutter, cut out 12 rounds, rerolling scraps as necessary. Press 1 round into each well of 12-count muffin pan. Refrigerate until chilled, about 30 minutes.

ALMOND STREUSEL: While dough is chilling, in bowl, whisk flour with sugar. Using pastry blender or 2 knives, cut in butter until mixture is crumbly and holds together in big clumps, using fingertips to blend if necessary. Stir in almonds. Set aside.

ASSEMBLY: Spoon rounded 1 tbsp of the jam into each pastry; top with almond streusel.

Bake on rimmed baking sheet in bottom third of 350°F (180°C) oven until pastry and streusel are light golden and filling is bubbly, 20 to 25 minutes. Let cool completely in pan. *(Make-ahead: Store in airtight container for up to 24 hours.)*

TIP FROM THE TEST KITCHEN
You can replace the cherry jam with any fruit jam.

NUTRITIONAL INFORMATION, PER MINI TART: about 308 cal, 3 g pro, 14 g total fat (7 g sat. fat), 44 g carb (1 g dietary fibre, 25 g sugar), 24 mg chol, 494 mg sodium, 66 mg potassium. % RDI: 2% calcium, 8% iron, 7% vit A, 5% vit C, 14% folate.

Mini Pumpkin Tarts

HANDS-ON TIME	•	TOTAL TIME	•	MAKES
35 MINUTES		4 HOURS		12 MINI TARTS

What you need

How to make it

PASTRY

1¼ cups	all-purpose flour
½ tsp	salt
¼ cup	cold unsalted butter, cubed
¼ cup	cold lard or vegetable shortening, cubed
1	egg yolk
2 tbsp	ice water (approx)
1½ tbsp	sour cream

FILLING

2½ cups	pumpkin purée
¼ cup	whipping cream (35%)
⅓ cup	packed brown sugar
2	eggs
½ tsp	cinnamon
¼ tsp	each ground ginger and vanilla
pinch	each ground cloves, nutmeg and salt

GARNISH

½ cup	whipping cream (35%)
1 tbsp	icing sugar
	freshly grated nutmeg

PASTRY: In large bowl, whisk flour with salt. Using pastry blender or 2 knives, cut in butter and lard until mixture resembles coarse crumbs with a few larger pieces.

In separate bowl, whisk together egg yolk, ice water and sour cream; drizzle over flour mixture, tossing with fork to form ragged dough and adding up to 1 tsp more ice water if necessary. Shape into disc; wrap in plastic wrap. Refrigerate until chilled, about 1 hour. *(Make-ahead: Refrigerate for up to 3 days or freeze for up to 1 month.)*

On lightly floured work surface, roll out dough to generous ⅛-inch (3 mm) thickness. Using 3¾-inch (10 cm) round cutter, cut out 12 rounds, rerolling scraps as necessary. Press 1 round into each well of 12-count muffin pan. Refrigerate until chilled, about 30 minutes.

FILLING: While dough is chilling, in bowl, beat together pumpkin, cream, brown sugar, eggs, cinnamon, ginger, vanilla, cloves, nutmeg and salt. Divide among pastry shells.

Bake in 350°F (180°C) oven until filling is set and slightly puffed, about 30 minutes. Let cool completely in pan. Refrigerate until chilled, about 1 hour. Remove from pan. *(Make-ahead: Refrigerate in airtight container for up to 24 hours.)*

GARNISH: In bowl, beat cream with icing sugar until stiff peaks form; spoon 4 tsp onto each tart. Sprinkle with nutmeg.

NUTRITIONAL INFORMATION, PER MINI TART: about 227 cal, 4 g pro, 15 g total fat (8 g sat. fat), 20 g carb (2 g dietary fibre, 8 g sugar), 81 mg chol, 119 mg sodium, 154 mg potassium. % RDI: 4% calcium, 11% iron, 71% vit A, 2% vit C, 13% folate.

Frozen Nanaimo Pie

HANDS-ON TIME	•	TOTAL TIME	•	MAKES
20 MINUTES		2¾ HOURS		8 TO 10 SERVINGS

What you need

¾ cup	graham cracker crumbs
⅓ cup	each sweetened shredded coconut and finely chopped walnuts
¼ cup	each cocoa powder and granulated sugar
⅓ cup	butter, melted
2 tbsp	custard powder (such as Bird's Traditional)
4 cups	French vanilla ice cream, softened
55 g	semisweet chocolate (about 2 oz), chopped
¼ cup	whipping cream (35%)

How to make it

In bowl, stir together graham crumbs, coconut, walnuts, cocoa powder and sugar. Drizzle with butter and stir until combined. Press into bottom and up side of 9-inch (23 cm) pie plate.

Fold custard powder into ice cream; spread over crust, smoothing top. Cover surface directly with plastic wrap; freeze until firm, 2 to 3 hours.

In small saucepan, heat chocolate and cream over medium-low heat, stirring occasionally, until melted and smooth. Let cool for 5 minutes. Spread over top of pie; freeze until firm, about 20 minutes. *(Make-ahead: Once firm, cover with plastic wrap and freeze for up to 24 hours.)* Let stand for 5 minutes before slicing.

TIP FROM THE TEST KITCHEN
To cut the pie easily, run your knife under warm water before slicing, and wipe it clean between slices.

NUTRITIONAL INFORMATION, PER EACH OF 10 SERVINGS: about 332 cal, 4 g pro, 21 g total fat (12 g sat. fat), 34 g carb (2 g dietary fibre, 25 g sugar), 47 mg chol, 170 mg sodium, 233 mg potassium. % RDI: 8% calcium, 9% iron, 14% vit A, 6% folate.

The Ultimate Peach Pie

HANDS-ON TIME
35 MINUTES

TOTAL TIME
2½ HOURS

MAKES
8 SERVINGS

What you need

PASTRY

2 cups	all-purpose flour
3 tbsp	cornmeal
½ tsp	salt
½ cup	cold butter, cubed
½ cup	cold lard, cubed
¼ cup	ice water (approx)
3 tbsp	sour cream

FILLING

6 cups	sliced pitted peeled firm ripe peaches
¾ cup	granulated sugar
¼ cup	all-purpose flour
1 tbsp	lemon juice
1 tsp	vanilla
1	egg yolk
2 tsp	coarse sugar (optional)

How to make it

PASTRY: In large bowl, whisk together flour, cornmeal and salt. Using pastry blender or 2 knives, cut in butter and lard until mixture resembles fine crumbs.

In separate bowl, whisk ice water with sour cream; drizzle over flour mixture, stirring briskly with fork to form ragged dough and adding more ice water, 1 tbsp at a time, until dough comes together. Divide pastry in half; press into discs. Wrap each in plastic wrap; refrigerate until chilled, about 30 minutes. *(Make-ahead: Refrigerate for up to 3 days.)*

FILLING: In bowl, combine peaches, granulated sugar, flour, lemon juice and vanilla; set aside.

ASSEMBLY: On lightly floured work surface, roll out 1 of the pastry discs to generous ⅛-inch (3 mm) thickness; fit pastry into 9-inch (23 cm) pie plate. Trim to fit, leaving ¾-inch (2 cm) overhang; flute rim. Spoon in peach mixture.

Roll out remaining pastry disc to scant ⅛-inch (3 mm) thickness. Using 2½-inch (6 cm) round pastry cutter, cut out about 24 circles, rerolling scraps as necessary. Cover peach mixture with circles, overlapping slightly, using about 15 for outer ring, about 8 for inner ring and 1 in centre. Whisk egg yolk with 2 tsp water; brush over circles and rim. Sprinkle with coarse sugar (if using). Bake on rimmed baking sheet on bottom rack of 425°F (220°C) oven for 20 minutes.

Reduce heat to 350°F (180°C); bake until bottom is golden brown, peaches are tender and juice is thick and bubbly, 60 to 70 minutes. Let cool on rack..

NUTRITIONAL INFORMATION, PER SERVING: about 385 cal, 5 g pro, 19 g total fat (9 g sat. fat), 52 g carb (3 g dietary fibre, 30 g sugar), 43 mg chol, 158 mg sodium, 285 mg potassium. % RDI: 2% calcium, 11% iron, 11% vit A, 10% vit C, 20% folate.

Maple Pots de Crème With Warm Pears

HANDS-ON TIME	•	TOTAL TIME	•	MAKES
30 MINUTES		5¼ HOURS		8 SERVINGS

What you need

MAPLE CUSTARD

1½ cups	each whipping cream (35%) and milk
⅓ cup	maple syrup
4	egg yolks
2	eggs
½ cup	granulated sugar
½ tsp	maple extract

WARM PEAR TOPPING

2 tbsp	butter
2	firm ripe Bosc or Bartlett pears, peeled, cored and diced (about 2½ cups total)
2 tbsp	maple syrup

How to make it

MAPLE CUSTARD: In saucepan, heat together cream, milk and maple syrup over medium heat just until bubbles form around edge.

In bowl, whisk together egg yolks, eggs and sugar until smooth; slowly whisk in cream mixture. Strain through fine-mesh sieve into pitcher; stir in maple extract. Pour into eight 6-oz (175 mL) ramekins. Place ramekins in roasting pan; pour in enough boiling water to come 1 inch (2.5 cm) up sides. Cover pan with foil.

Bake in 325°F (160°C) oven until edges are lightly set yet centres still jiggle slightly, 30 to 35 minutes. Transfer ramekins to rack; let cool completely. Cover with plastic wrap and refrigerate until chilled, about 4 hours. (Make-ahead: Refrigerate for up to 2 days.)

WARM PEAR TOPPING: While custard is chilling, in skillet, melt butter over medium-high heat; cook pears, stirring often, until browned and softened, about 6 minutes. Stir in maple syrup; cook, stirring, until pears are coated, about 1 minute. Scrape into bowl. Let cool to room temperature. Serve over custard.

TIP FROM THE TEST KITCHEN

If you're unsure of whether the custard is set, insert the tip of a sharp knife into the centre. If the knife comes out clean, the custard is done.

NUTRITIONAL INFORMATION, PER SERVING: about 360 cal, 5 g pro, 23 g total fat (13 g sat. fat), 34 g carb (1 g dietary fibre, 30 g sugar), 213 mg chol, 80 mg sodium, 209 mg potassium. % RDI: 11% calcium, 6% iron, 27% vit A, 2% vit C, 12% folate.

White Chocolate Mousse
With Passion Fruit and Coconut Chips

HANDS-ON TIME	•	TOTAL TIME	•	MAKES
15 MINUTES		5 HOURS		8 SERVINGS

What you need

3 cups	whipping cream (35%)
400 g	white chocolate (about 14 oz), chopped
2 tsp	unflavoured gelatin
4	passion fruits
¾ cup	coconut chips

How to make it

In saucepan, heat 1½ cups of the cream over medium-low heat until bubbles form around edge. Stir in chocolate until melted.

Meanwhile, in small microwaveable bowl, add 2 tbsp water; sprinkle gelatin over top. Let stand until absorbed, about 2 minutes. Microwave on high until gelatin is dissolved, about 10 seconds. Whisk into chocolate mixture. Scrape into clean bowl; refrigerate until room temperature, stirring occasionally, about 30 minutes.

Beat remaining cream until stiff peaks form; fold into chocolate mixture. Pour into eight 1-cup (250 mL) serving dishes. Refrigerate until set, about 4 hours (*Make-ahead: Cover and refrigerate for up to 2 days.*)

Cut passion fruits in half; scoop out pulp. Top mousse with pulp and coconut chips.

TIP FROM THE TEST KITCHEN
Dissolved gelatin doesn't take long to set once it's mixed with a cooler substance, so whisk it into the chocolate mixture quickly.

NUTRITIONAL INFORMATION, PER SERVING: about 608 cal, 6 g pro, 50 g total fat (31 g sat. fat), 38 g carb (2 g dietary fibre, 33 g sugar), 117 mg chol, 81 mg sodium, 284 mg potassium. % RDI: 15% calcium, 3% iron, 32% vit A, 7% vit C, 5% folate.

Sour Cherry Trifle

HANDS-ON TIME	•	TOTAL TIME	•	MAKES
45 MINUTES		3 HOURS		10 TO 12 SERVINGS

What you need | How to make it

CUSTARD

5	egg yolks
⅓ cup	granulated sugar
3 tbsp	cornstarch
2 cups	whole milk
3 tbsp	butter
½ tsp	vanilla

CAKE

1	sponge cake (9 inch/23 cm)
¼ cup	raspberry jam or strawberry jam
⅔ cup	sweet sherry or Madeira

TOPPING

1	jar (796 mL) red sour cherries in light syrup
⅓ cup	granulated sugar
1¼ cups	crumbled amaretti cookies
1½ cups	whipping cream (35%)
¼ cup	sliced almonds, toasted

CUSTARD: In bowl, whisk together egg yolks, sugar and cornstarch. In saucepan, heat milk over medium heat just until bubbles form around edge; gradually whisk one-third of the milk into egg mixture. Whisk back into pan and cook over medium heat, whisking constantly, until mixture comes to a boil. Continue to cook, whisking, until bubbling and thickened, 3 to 4 minutes. Remove from heat. Whisk in butter and vanilla. Place plastic wrap directly on surface; let cool slightly.

CAKE: While custard is cooling, cut cake in half horizontally. Spread cut side of bottom with jam; replace top half, pressing to adhere. Cut into about 1-inch (2.5 cm) cubes.

Line 12-cup (3 L) trifle bowl with half of the cake pieces; brush with half of the sherry. Repeat with remaining cake pieces and sherry. Scrape warm custard over top; place plastic wrap directly on surface. Refrigerate until chilled, about 2 hours.

TOPPING: While cake mixture is chilling, in saucepan, bring cherries with syrup and sugar to boil over medium-high heat; boil until syrupy and reduced by half, about 25 minutes. Transfer to bowl; let cool. Refrigerate until cold, about 1 hour.

Transfer cherry mixture to strainer set over bowl; let stand for 10 minutes to drain. Reserve liquid.

Sprinkle amaretti over custard. Spoon cherry mixture over top; drizzle with 2 tbsp of the reserved cherry liquid.

In bowl, beat cream until peaks form; spread over trifle. Sprinkle with almonds.

NUTRITIONAL INFORMATION, PER EACH OF 12 SERVINGS:
about 456 cal, 7 g pro, 20 g total fat (11 g sat. fat), 61 g carb, 2 g dietary fibre, 175 mg chol, 176 mg sodium, 211 mg potassium. % RDI: 11% calcium, 14% iron, 23% vit A, 3% vit C, 16% folate.

Pumpkin Amaretti Mousse

p.152

HANDS-ON TIME	TOTAL TIME	MAKES
20 MINUTES	2¼ HOURS	8 SERVINGS

What you need

½ cup	granulated sugar
1 cup	pumpkin purée
1 cup	10% plain Mediterranean-style yogurt
1 tsp	cinnamon
½ tsp	each ground ginger and vanilla
pinch	each ground cloves and nutmeg
1⅓ cups	whipping cream (35%)
2	amaretti cookies, cut in crumbs (about ¼ cup)

How to make it

Set aside 1 tbsp of the sugar. In food processor, blend together pumpkin, yogurt, the remaining sugar, cinnamon, ginger, vanilla, cloves and nutmeg until smooth; scrape into large bowl.

Whip 1 cup of the cream with reserved sugar until stiff peaks form; fold into pumpkin mixture. Spoon into 8 small cups or ramekins; cover with plastic wrap and refrigerate until set, about 2 hours. *(Make-ahead: Refrigerate for up to 2 days.)*

Whip remaining cream until stiff peaks form. Spoon over mousse; sprinkle with amaretti crumbs.

NUTRITIONAL INFORMATION, PER SERVING: about 239 cal, 3 g pro, 17 g total fat (11 g sat. fat), 20 g carb (1 g dietary fibre, 17 g sugar), 63 mg chol, 39 mg sodium, 165 mg potassium. % RDI: 8% calcium, 4% iron, 56% vit A, 2% vit C, 2% folate.

Chocolate Caramel Cupcake Parfaits
p.6

HANDS-ON TIME	TOTAL TIME	MAKES
20 MINUTES	2 HOURS	6 SERVINGS

What you need

How to make it

CHOCOLATE CUPCAKES

¾ cup	all-purpose flour
½ cup	granulated sugar
3 tbsp	cocoa powder, sifted
½ tsp	baking soda
pinch	salt
¼ cup	vegetable oil
½ tsp	vanilla
2 tsp	white or cider vinegar

CARAMEL SAUCE

¼ cup	butter
⅓ cup	granulated sugar
1 tsp	lemon juice
¼ cup	whipping cream (35%)

VANILLA WHIPPED CREAM

half	vanilla bean
1 cup	whipping cream (35%)
1 tbsp	icing sugar

GARNISH

1	chocolate-covered toffee bar (such as Skor), chopped

CHOCOLATE CUPCAKES: In large bowl, whisk together flour, sugar, cocoa powder, baking soda and salt; whisk in oil, vanilla and ½ cup water. Stir in vinegar. Divide among 6 paper-lined muffin cups.

Bake in 350°F (180°C) oven until cake tester inserted in centres comes out clean, about 18 minutes. Cool in pan for 10 minutes; transfer directly to rack to cool completely. *(Make-ahead: Store in airtight container for up to 24 hours.)*

CARAMEL SAUCE: While cupcakes are baking, in saucepan, cook butter, sugar and lemon juice over medium heat, stirring, until butter is melted and sugar is dissolved. Continue to cook, without stirring, until light amber in colour, 4 to 5 minutes.

Remove from heat; standing back and averting face, stir in cream. Pour into heatproof bowl; let cool until lukewarm, about 45 minutes.

VANILLA WHIPPED CREAM: While caramel is cooling, using paring knife, halve vanilla bean lengthwise. Scrape seeds into bowl; pour in cream. Beat in icing sugar until stiff peaks form.

ASSEMBLY: Using serrated knife, cut cupcakes horizontally into thirds. Place 1 bottom third, cut side up, into each of 6 serving glasses; drizzle each with heaping 1 tsp of the caramel sauce. Spoon heaping 1 tbsp of the whipped cream over top. Repeat layers twice. *(Make-ahead: Cover parfaits and remaining caramel with plastic wrap; refrigerate for up to 24 hours.)* Drizzle with remaining caramel.

GARNISH: Sprinkle parfaits with toffee bar pieces.

NUTRITIONAL INFORMATION, PER SERVING: about 523 cal, 4 g pro, 37 g total fat (18 g sat. fat), 47 g carb (1 g dietary fibre, 33 g sugar), 87 mg chol, 200 mg sodium, 139 mg potassium. % RDI: 4% calcium, 9% iron, 25% vit A, 12% folate.

Pumpkin Amaretti Mousse
page 150

INDEX

🍃 = Vegetarian

Index

◣ = Vegetarian

Index

🍂 = Vegetarian

◗ = Vegetarian

Savoury Cheddar Cheesecake Spread
page 11

CREDITS

RECIPES

All recipes were developed by the Canadian Living Test Kitchen

PHOTOGRAPHY

RYAN BROOK p. 91, 100 and 105.

JEFF COULSON back cover (bread and cake); p. 16, 42, 59, 73, 80, 117, 121, 126, 130, 13, 142, 152 and 159.

YVONNE DUIVENVOORDEN p. 129.

JOE KIM p. 69.

STEVE KRUG p. 4.

JODI PUDGE front cover; back cover (ribs and sandwich); p. 21, 29, 35, 41, 50, 63, 79, 86, 95, 96, 106, 122 and 149.

RYAN SZULC p. 64, 70, 74 and 141.

RONALD TSANG back cover (soup); p. 6, 30, 49, 85 and 146.

JAMES TSE back cover (tart); p. 36, 55, 56, 113, 136 and 145.

MAYA VISYEI p. 9 and 125.

FOOD STYLING

ANDREW CHASE p. 64 and 70.

ASHLEY DENTON front cover; p. 35, 41, 69, 96 and 117.

MICHAEL ELLIOTT/JUDY INC. back cover (ribs and sandwich); p. 6, 8, 21, 36, 49, 50, 55, 56, 63, 79, 146 and 149.

IRENE FONG p. 91

DAVID GRENIER p. 16, 29, 74, 80, 106, 145 and 152.

MIRANDA KEYES p. 59.

MATTHEW KIMURA p. 130.

LUCIE RICHARD back cover (tart); p. 136.

CHRISTOPHER ST ONGE back cover (soup); p. 30, 42, 85 and 113.

CLAIRE STUBBS p. 86, 95, 125 and 129.

MELANIE STUPARYK p. 100, 126, 135 and 159.

NOAH WITENOFF back cover (cake); p. 4, 105, 121, 122 and 142.

NICOLE YOUNG back cover (bread); p. 73 and 141.

PROP STYLING

LAURA BRANSON back cover (tart); p. 6, 49, 59, 69, 117, 136, 145 and 146.

AURELIE BRYCE p. 126 and 152.

ALANNA DAVEY back cover (soup); p. 85 and 129.

CATHERINE DOHERTY back cover (ribs and sandwich); p. 21, 50, 63, 79, 91, 100, 125 and 149.

JENNIFER EVANS front cover; p. 4, 8, 29, 30, 35, 36, 41, 55, 56, 96, 106 and 113.

MANDY GYULAY p. 86 and 95.

MADELEINE JOHARI back cover (bread and cake); p. 64, 70, 73, 74, 105, 121, 135, 141 and 159.

SABRINA LINN p. 16, 80 and 142.

SASHA SEYMOUR p. 42 and 130.

CHARLENE WALTON/JUDY INC. p. 122 .

Bok Choy and
Fennel Slaw
page 99

About Our Nutrition Information

To meet nutrient needs each day, moderately active women aged 25 to 49 need about 1,900 calories, 51 g protein, 261 g carbohydrate, 25 to 35 g fibre and not more than 63 g total fat (21 g saturated fat). Men and teenagers usually need more. Canadian sodium intake of approximately 3,500 mg daily should be reduced, whereas the intake of potassium from food sources should be increased to 4,700 mg per day. The percentage of recommended daily intake (% RDI) is based on the values used for Canadian food labels for calcium, iron, vitamins A and C, and folate.

Figures are rounded off. They are based on the first ingredient listed when there is a choice and do not include optional ingredients or those with no specified amounts.

ABBREVIATIONS

cal = calories
pro = protein
carb = carbohydrate
sat. fat = saturated fat
chol = cholesterol

Canadian Living

Complete your collection of Tested-Till-Perfect recipes!